THE WORKS OF ARISTOTLE

THE WORKS OF ARISTOTLE

TRANSLATED INTO ENGLISH UNDER THE EDITORSHIP

OF

SIR DAVID ROSS

VOLUME XII

SELECT FRAGMENTS

ISBN: 978-93-5128-728-5(PB)

First Published in 1952
Indian Reprint in 2017

Published by

Kalpaz Publications
C-30, Satyawati Nagar,
Delhi – 110052
E-mail: kalpaz@hotmail.com
Website: kalpazpublications.com
Ph.: +91-9212142040

Cataloging in Publication Data—DK
Courtesy: D.K. Agencies (P) Ltd. <docinfo@dkagencies.com>

Aristotle, author.
[Fragments. Selections. English]
The works of Aristotle. Volume XII, Select fragments / translated into English under the editorship of Sir David Ross.
pages cm
Translated from Greek.
"First published in 1952"—Title page verso.
Includes bibliographical references and index.
ISBN 9789351287285

1. Philosophy, Ancient. I. Ross, W. D. (William David), 1877-1971, translator. II. Title. III. Title: Select fragments.

PA3893.Z5F73 2017 DDC 185 23

PREFACE

It was suggested to me many years ago by Prof. A. E. Taylor that a translation of some of the fragments of Aristotle's lost works would be a useful addition to the Oxford Translation of the extant works. I then thought that I had enough on my hands without this addition. In the interval, however, interest in the fragments has been quickened by the pioneer work of such scholars as Prof. Jaeger, Prof. Bignone, and Prof. Wilpert, and many passages not included in Rose's editions of the fragments have been recognized as being derived from Aristotle's lost works.

A translation of the whole of the fragments included by Rose would not be of much general interest, and I have thought it best to limit this selection to three of the sections in his editions—the dialogues, the logical works, and the philosophical works. The references in the notes to this translation are to the page and line of Rose's Teubner edition. At the same time I have included many other passages which have been with probability assigned to Aristotle by the scholars named above and others. I must in particular express my indebtedness to Dr. R. Walzer, who has not only published a useful edition of some of the fragments, but has called my attention to others which would otherwise have escaped my notice, and has lent me some useful books and articles.

It is not intended to make any further addition to the Oxford Translation of Aristotle.

W. D. R.

TABLE OF CONTENTS

INTRODUCTION	vii
DIALOGUES	1–102
Gryllus, or *On Rhetoric*	7
Symposium	8–14
Sophistes	15
Eudemus, or *On Soul*	16–23
Nerinthus	24
Eroticus	25–26
Protrepticus	27–56
On Wealth	57
On Prayer	58
On Good Birth	59–62
On Pleasure	63
On Education	64
On Kingship	65–66
Alexander	67
Politicus	68–71
On Poets	72–77
On Philosophy	78–99
On Justice	100–2
LOGICAL WORKS	103–14
On Problems	104
Divisions	105
Dissertations	106
Categories	107–8
On Contraries	109–14
PHILOSOPHICAL WORKS	115–49
On the Good	115–23
On Ideas	124–33
On the Pythagoreans	134–46
On the Philosophy of Archytas	147
On Democritus	148–9

CONTENTS

AUTHORS QUOTED 150

ROSE'S NUMBERING OF FRAGMENTS 155

BIBLIOGRAPHY 156

INDEX 161

INTRODUCTION

THE oldest lists of Aristotle's works that have come down to us from antiquity are those written by Diogenes Laertius, in the third century A.D., and by Hesychius, probably in the fifth. A strong case has been made out by E. Howald[1] for the view that both lists rest on the good authority of Hermippus (about 200 B.C.).

Diogenes' list begins as follows:

On Justice, 4 books[2]
On Poets, 3 books[3]
On Philosophy, 3 books[4]
Politicus, 2 books[5]
On Rhetoric, or *Gryllus*, 1 book[6]
Nerinthus, 1 book
Sophistes, 1 book
Menexenus, 1 book
Eroticus, 1 book
Symposium, 1 book[7]
On Wealth, 1 book
Protrepticus, 1 book
On Soul,[8] 1 book
On Prayer, 1 book
On Good Birth,[9] 1 book

[1] In *Hermes*, 1920, 204–21.

[2] Cicero, p. 100 *infra*, refers to its four books; Suetonius, p. 100 *infra*, refers to the first book.

[3] Diogenes Laertius, p. 73 *infra*, refers to book 1; Macrobius, p. 75 *infra*, to book 2; Ps.-Plutarch, p. 76 *infra*, to book 3.

[4] Hesychius says '4 books'; Syrianus, p. 83 *infra*, refers to book 2; Philodemus, p. 78 *infra*, and Cicero, p. 97 *infra*, refer to book 3.

[5] πολιτικοῦ ᾱ β 4 MSS. of Diogenes; περὶ πολιτικοῦ 1 MS. of Diogenes; πολιτικόν ᾱ Hesychius. Syrianus, p. 68 *infra*, refers to the second book.

[6] '3 books', Hesychius.

[7] From pp. 11–14 *infra* we may *infer* that this work was also known as the work *On Drunkenness*.

[8] We learn from Plutarch, pp. 16, 18 *infra*, and from Simplicius, p. 21 *infra*, that this was also called *Eudemus*.

[9] Plutarch says, p. 60 *infra*, that the genuineness of this work is doubtful,

On Pleasure, 1 book
Alexander, or *On Colonists*,[1] 1 book
On Kingship, 1 book
On Education, 1 book.

The list goes on to

On the Good, 3 books
From Plato's Laws, 3 books
From the Republic, 2 books
On Economy, 1 book
On Friendship, 1 book,

and so on.

It is clear that the first nineteen works in Diogenes' list formed for him a separate group, arranged according to the number of books each work contained, and that from it he went on to a second group similarly arranged. The same nineteen works appear at the beginning of Hesychius' list, except that the *Alexander* appears a little later and its place is taken by the *Economicus*.

Some of these works are known to have been dialogues. The works *On Poets, On Philosophy*, and *On Soul* (or *Eudemus*) are explicitly so described by ancient authors.[2] The form of *Politicus* fr. 1, *Eudemus* fr. 6, and *On Good Birth* frs. 1, 2, 4 shows that these were dialogues. Themistius' reference to 'the Corinthian dialogue'[3] is usually taken to refer to the *Nerinthus*. The *Historia Augusta* says that Cicero's *Hortensius* was modelled on the *Protrepticus*,[4] and as the *Hortensius* was a dialogue[5] the *Protrepticus* was probably one too. There is thus good evidence that several of the nineteen works that stand at the head of Diogenes' and Hesychius' lists were dialogues; it may be inferred with high probability, though not with certainty, that the others were so too.

but Stobaeus, pp. 59, 61 *infra*, and Athenaeus, p. 61 *infra*, confirm its genuineness.

[1] Diogenes has ὑπὲρ ἀποίκων, Hesychius ὑπὲρ ἀποικιῶν, which is more probable. But if, as is likely, ὑπέρ is used in the sense of 'about', the subtitle probably does not go back to Aristotle, who rarely uses ὑπέρ in this sense.

[2] For *On Poets*, see p. 72 *infra*; for *On Philosophy*, pp. 78, 82 *infra*; for the *Eudemus*, pp. 19–22 *infra*.

[3] See p. 24 *infra*. [4] See p. 27 *infra*. [5] See pp. 41, 42, 46 *infra*.

It seems probable that Aristotle began with short dialogues called (on the Platonic model) by one-word names (three of which are actually identical with the names of Platonic dialogues), that from these he proceeded to works which were still dialogues but began to have something of the character of treatises and are therefore designated as 'on' so-and-so, and later still went on to the large works containing more than one book. Thus we get, tentatively, three groups:

1. *Menexenus, Symposium, Sophistes, Nerinthus, Eroticus, Gryllus, Eudemus, Protrepticus, Alexander.*
2. *On Wealth, On Prayer, On Good Birth, On Pleasure, On Kingship, On Education.*
3. *Politicus, On Poets, On Philosophy, On Justice.*

Before we make any further attempt to date the dialogues, it is necessary to have in mind the various periods of Aristotle's life. From his eighteenth year to his thirty-seventh (367–348/7) he was a member of the school of Plato at Athens. The next five years he spent partly at Assos, in Mysia, and partly at Mitylene, in Lesbos. From 343/2 to about 340 he was in Macedonia, tutoring Alexander the Great, and for about five years thereafter he was pursuing his studies in his native town, Stagira. From 335/4 till his death in 323 he was actively engaged as the head of his own school, the Lyceum, in Athens.

We must make one alteration in our tentative grouping. The work *Alexander*, or *On Colonists*, is, as Jaeger has pointed out, suitable only to the time at which Alexander was engaged in setting up colonies in Asia, from (say) 331 B.C. onwards, while the work *On Kingship* (also addressed to Alexander) can most suitably be dated at or before Alexander's succession to the throne in 336. Thus the work *Alexander* must be removed from the first group, and placed later than *On Kingship* in the second group.

The *Gryllus* must be dated after the death of Gryllus at the battle of Mantinea in 362/1,[1] but probably not very long after it. It may therefore well be the earliest of all Aristotle's works; it is worth while to note that he had a model for it

[1] See p. 7 *infra*.

in Plato's *Gorgias*.[1] The *Eudemus* must be dated after, but probably not long after, the death of Eudemus in 354/3. Thus these two works, at least, probably belong to the time of Aristotle's membership of the Academy, while the work *On Kingship* and the *Alexander* belong to the period 343–331. The date of the *Protrepticus* has been examined by B. Einarson and by P. Von der Mühll in the articles mentioned in our bibliography. On the basis of connexions between the dialogue and Isocrates' *Antidosis*, Einarson has argued for a date shortly after, and Von der Mühll for a date shortly before, 353, and it is likely that one or other of these scholars is right. The work *On Philosophy*, in which Aristotle vigorously attacked Plato's theory of Ideas, must have been written after Plato's death and Aristotle's withdrawal from the Academy. With regard to the rest of the dialogues we cannot be certain whether they were written during or after Aristotle's membership of the Academy; but it is probable that most of them were written during it; for the remaining twenty-five years of his life are none too long to serve for the task of founding and directing the Peripatetic school, and of composing the vast fabric of the complete works that have survived to our day, and the very many lost works other than dialogues that are named in the ancient lists of his works.

There is an important point of form in which some of Aristotle's dialogues differed from Plato's. Plato never appears as a speaker in any of his dialogues. Cicero in one passage[2] speaks of 'the Aristotelian plan, in which the parts are so assigned to others that the writer himself has the principal part'. But in another passage[3] he describes his own *De Oratore* as Aristotelian in method, though he is not in that work the chief speaker. Aristotle's practice, therefore, must have varied. The only dialogue in which it is certain that he must have appeared as a speaker himself is the *Politicus*, in which Cicero says expressly[4] that he did so. But there are phrases in fragments from the *Eudemus*[5] and the work *On*

[1] As he had for the *Eudemus* in the *Phaedo*, and for the *Protrepticus* in the *Euthydemus*. [2] *Att.* 13. 19. 4, p. 3 *infra*. [3] *Fam.* 1. 9. 23, p. 3 *infra*.
[4] *Q. Fr.* 3. 5. 1, p. 68 *infra*. [5] fr. 2, p. 17 *infra*.

Philosophy[1] which suggest that there too Aristotle appeared in person.

In his *Aristoteles Pseudepigraphus* and in his Berlin edition of the fragments Rose included the work *On Kingship* and the *Alexander* among the dialogues (for him, the pseudo-Aristotelian dialogues), but in his Teubner edition he places these works partly among the speeches and partly among the letters; in the latter case his ground seems to have been the occurrence of the phrase τῶν ἀπεσταλκότων ('the senders') in an extract from Strabo.[2] In this he was mistaken. Diogenes expressly distinguishes these two works, which come in the first section of his list of Aristotle's works, from the four volumes of letters to Alexander, which come near the end of the list; and Hesychius places the two works near the beginning of his list, but the letters to Alexander among the pseudographa at the end of his life. The phrase 'the senders' proves nothing; a dialogue, no less than a letter, might have been sent to Alexander. The pseudo-Ammonius distinguishes the two works in question from the letters,[3] and describes the work *On Kingship* as a single-volume book;[4] and Cicero also calls it a book.[5]

Rose includes among the dialogues the work *On the Good* and the *Magicus*. But there is ample evidence that the former was not a dialogue, but Aristotle's record of Plato's famous lectures on the Good. As for the *Magicus*, Suidas s.v. Ἀντισθένης says that some people assign it to Aristotle, but he himself assigns it to Antisthenes; it occurs nowhere in Diogenes' list, and in Hesychius' list only at the end, in a list of works which he describes as spurious.

Of the works other than dialogues included in our selection, the most important were those *On the Good* and *On Ideas*. The former was Aristotle's record of the lectures in which Plato unfolded the latest phase of his theory of Ideas, the theory of Ideal numbers; and every fragment of it that we possess is of interest as helping to give us some understanding of that mysterious theory. Again, the researches of Jaeger and Wilpert have shown that the criticism of the ideal theory

[1] frs. 10, 11, pp. 82, 83 *infra*. [2] p. 67 *infra*.
[3] p. 65 *infra*. [4] p. 65 *infra*. [5] p. 65 *infra*.

in *Metaphysics* A. 9 is in all probability based on an earlier and much fuller criticism in the work *On Ideas*, which, with the work *On Philosophy*, formed Aristotle's earliest expression of his breakaway from the Platonic system. Wilpert has been able to show that much more of *On the Good* and *On Ideas* (and also of *On the Pythagoreans*) can be recovered from the pages of the Greek commentators on Aristotle than had previously been recognized.

The best existing commentary on the *Eudemus*, the *Protrepticus*, and the work *On Philosophy* is to be found in Jaeger's *Aristoteles*.

The ransacking of ancient literature to find fragments of Aristotle has been carried further by E. Bignone in many articles catalogued in our Bibliography, and in his massive work *L'Aristotele Perduto e la Formazione Filosofica di Epicuro*. It is doubtful whether Greek or Latin literature has much more to yield in this kind. More is to be expected from the still unexplored field of Arabic literature on philosophy, and here a beginning has been made by R. Walzer (see pp. 23, 26 *infra*), who has also published a scholarly text of the fragments of the *Eudemus*, the *Protrepticus*, and the work *On Philosophy*.

In our numbering of the fragments, 'R^2' refers to Rose's Berlin edition, 'R^3' to his Leipzig edition, 'W' to Walzer's edition. In the notes on readings, 'R' refers to Rose's Leipzig edition.

DIALOGUES

TESTIMONIA

ARIST. *Ph.* 194^a35–36: see p. 99 *infra*.

ARIST. *De An.* 404^b18–21: see p. 83 *infra*.

ARIST. *Poet.* 1454^b15–18. All these rules one must keep in mind throughout, and further, those also for such points of stage-effect as directly depend on the art of the poet, since in these, too, one may often make mistakes. Enough, however, has been said on the subject in our published writings.[1]

CIC. *Inv.* 2. 2. 6. Aristotle so greatly excelled in charm and brevity of speech the inventors of rhetoric themselves, that no one knows their precepts from their own books, but all who wish to understand their precepts return to him as to an expositor much more suited to their needs.

CIC. *De Or.* 1. 11. 49. For this reason, if the natural philosopher Democritus was eloquent (as is commonly held and as I myself think), while his matter was that of a natural philosopher his eloquence must be deemed to be that of an orator. And if Plato has, as I admit, spoken like a god about matters far removed from political controversy—if Aristotle, Theophrastus, and Carneades were, on the subjects they discussed, eloquent, charming, and polished in their language—then, though the subjects they discuss belong to other studies, their language itself belongs to this single art which we are speaking about and inquiring into.

Ibid. 3. 21. 80. But if anyone ever comes forward who can, in the Aristotelian manner, put forward both sides on every subject, and can with knowledge of Aristotle's precepts

[1] i.e. in the dialogue *On Poets*.

develop two contrary speeches on every question, or who can in the manner of Arcesilaus and Carneades argue against any proposition that is put forward, and who adds to that method this practice and training in speaking, let us agree that he is the true, the perfect, the only orator.

CIC. *Brut.* 31. 120–1. For this reason I approve all the more of your judgement, Brutus, in following the Academic school, in whose doctrine and precepts methodical discussion is united with charm and fluency of speech; although that very practice of the Peripatetics and Academics in the matter of speaking is such that, while there cannot be a perfect orator without it, it does not by itself make a perfect orator. For as the language of the Stoics is too terse and a little too much compressed to appeal to the ears of the public, so the language of those others is too free and expansive for the practice of the courts and the forum. Who is richer in style than Plato? The philosophers say Jove speaks so, if he speaks Greek. Who is more sinewy than Aristotle, more charming than Theophrastus?

CIC. *Top.* 1. 3. The obscurity of Aristotle's *Topics* has repelled you; and the great rhetorician replied, I fancy, that he did not know the works of Aristotle. I have, indeed, been very little surprised that a rhetorician did not know a philosopher who is unknown to philosophers themselves, all but a very few; for which they are the less to be pardoned because they ought to have been attracted not only by the things he has said and discovered, but also by the incredible fluency and charm of his style.

CIC. *Fin.* 5. 5. 12. Since there are two kinds of books, one written in popular style, and called by them exoteric, and another more precise kind which they left in the form of treatises, Aristotle and Theophrastus seem not to be always consistent with themselves on the subject of the supreme good.

CIC. *Lucullus* 38. 119 (Plasberg): see p. 92 *infra*.

CIC. *Fam.* 1. 9. 23. I have written, therefore, in the Aristotelian manner (at least that was what I wanted to do), three books in my discussion or dialogue *On the Orator*.

CIC. *Att.* 4. 16. 2. You know the style of my dialogues. . . . I have put into the mouths of Africanus, Philus, Laelius, and Manilius the discussion *On the State* which I have started; I have added some young men. . . . And so I planned, in having a preface in each book, as Aristotle does in the books which he calls exoteric, to do something that would justify me in appealing to him—which I believe will please you; heaven grant that I may complete my effort!

Ibid. 13. 19. 3–4. If I had represented Cotta and Varro as disputing with one another, as your last letter advises me to do, my rôle would have been a silent one. This has a good effect when characters from antiquity are introduced; Heraclides has used the device in many works, and we have done so in our six books *On the State*. There are also three books of ours *On the Orator* which I think very highly of; in those, too, the persons are such that it was right for me to be silent. . . . I am supposed to be a boy when that dialogue starts, so that I could have no part of my own. But what I have *now* written follows the Aristotelian plan, in which the parts are so assigned to others that the writer himself has the principal part. I have completed in this manner five books *On Ends*.

CIC. *Q. Fr.* 3. 5. 1: see p. 68 *infra*.

QUINT. 10. 1. 83. What shall I say of Aristotle? I doubt whether I admire him more for his knowledge, for the copiousness of his writings, for the charm of his language, for his keenness of invention, or for the wide range of his works.

DIO CHR. *Or.* 53. 1. Indeed Aristotle himself, from whom they say criticism and grammar took their origin, discusses the poet in several dialogues, for the most part admiring and honouring him.

Plu. *Mor.* 447 f–448 a. Why is it that in philosophical inquiries the process of being led by others and often changing one's ground is not always painful, and that Aristotle himself, Democritus, and Chrysippus gave up without fuss or ill-feeling, and indeed with pleasure, some of their former opinions? It is because no passion opposes the part of the soul that contemplates and learns; in such cases the irrational part remains calm and does not concern itself, so that reason willingly turns towards the truth when it appears, and abandons what is untrue.

Ibid. 1115 b–c. With regard to the Ideas, about which Aristotle chides Plato, misrepresenting them completely and bringing every possible objection against them, in his ethical works, in his metaphysical works, in his physical works, in his popular dialogues, he seemed to some to be polemical rather than philosophical in his attitude towards this doctrine, as though his object was to belittle the Platonic philosophy; so far was he from following it.

Diog. *Oen.* fr. 4, col. 1. 7–col. 2. 8. When they say that things cannot be apprehended, what else are they saying than that we ought not to study nature; who will choose to look for what he can never find? Aristotle and the members of his school say nothing can be known, since owing to the mere speed of their fluxion things escape our apprehension.

Eus. *P.E.* 14. 6. 9–10. Cephisodorus, when he saw his master Isocrates being attacked by Aristotle, was ignorant of and unversed in Aristotle himself, but, seeing the repute which Plato's views enjoyed, he thought that Aristotle was following Plato; so he waged war on Aristotle but was really attacking Plato. His criticism began with the Ideas and finished with the other doctrines—things which he himself did not know; he was only guessing at the meaning of the opinions held about them. This Cephisodorus was not fighting the person he was attacking, but was fighting the person he did not wish to attack.[1]

[1] i.e. not Aristotle but Plato.

THEM. *Or.* 319 c. And so Aristotle's popular works, which are meant for the multitude, are full of light and translucent; their usefulness is not unmixed with enjoyment and pleasure; Aphrodite and the Graces blossom on them.

BASIL, *Ep.* 135. Even of secular philosophers those who wrote dialogues, Aristotle and Theophrastus, at once got to grips with the facts, because they were conscious of their lack of the Platonic graces.

AMM. *in Cat.* 6. 25–27. 4. We say that the Philosopher has evidently expressed his views in different ways. In the acroamatic works he is, as regards the thought, terse, compressed, and full of questions, and as regards the language quite ordinary, owing to his search for precise truth and clearness; he sometimes even invents words if necessary. In the dialogues, which he has written for the many, he aims at a certain fullness, a careful choice of diction and metaphor, and modifies the style of his diction to suit the speakers, and in short does everything that can beautify his style.

SIMP. *in Cat.* 4. 14. Of the general works, some are hypomnematic, viz. those which the philosopher put together to aid his own memory and with a view to submitting them to further testing. . . . 19–20. Alexander[1] says these works have been hastily put together and do not aim at one end; for which reason, and to distinguish them from these, he says the others are called systematic. Of these some are in dialogue form, while in others Aristotle speaks in his own person.

SIMP. *in De Caelo* 288. 31–289. 2. By 'popular philosophical discussions' Aristotle means those originally intended for the many, which we are wont also to call exoteric, as we call the more serious books acroamatic and systematic; Aristotle speaks of this in the books *On Philosophy*.

ELIAS *in Cat.* 114. 15. In some of his systematic works Aristotle speaks in his own person (and these are also called

[1] i.e. of Aphrodisias.

acroamatic), while others are in dialogue form, and are also called exoteric. The former class, as being works in which he speaks in his own person, are opposed to the dialogues, and as being acroamatic they are opposed to the exoteric works. For, wishing to benefit all men, Aristotle wrote both in his own person, for philosophical students . . . 22 and in dialogue form, for those who were not. In the acroamatic works, since he was addressing people who were prepared to think philosophically, he used conclusive arguments, while in the dialogues he used probable arguments. . . . 115. 3–5. Alexander mentions another difference between the acroamatic works and the dialogues, that in the former Aristotle says what he thinks and what is true, while in the latter he expresses the false opinions of others.

Ibid. 124. 3–6. In those of the general works which are dialogues, i.e. the exoteric works, he is clear, because he is arguing for non-philosophers, but because he is arguing among dialecticians he is versatile in his impersonations, full of Aphrodite and overflowing with the Graces.

GRYLLUS, or ON RHETORIC

1 (R^2 57, R^3 68)

DIOG. LAERT. 2. 6. 55. Aristotle says that a host of people wrote encomia and funeral speeches on Gryllus, partly in the wish to please his father.[1]

2 (R^2 58, R^3 69)

QUINT. *Inst.* 2. 17. 1. Let us pass, then, to the question that follows, whether rhetoric is an art. This . . . was not doubted by any of those who have handed down rules for oratory. . . . With these most of the Stoic and the Peripatetic philosophers agree. . . . 4. I, for my part, think that those who argued against this were not so much saying what they really thought as wishing to exercise their wits by dealing with a difficult subject. . . . 5. Some want rhetoric to be a natural gift. . . . 7. They maintain that nothing which proceeds from art can have existed before the art did . . . 11. that that which a man does without learning to do it has nothing to do with art, but that even men who have not learned to speak do speak. . . . 14. Aristotle, according to his wont, from sheer love of inquiry worked out in the *Gryllus* some arguments which show his usual subtlety. But he also wrote three books on the art of rhetoric, and in the first of them admits that rhetoric is not merely an art; he assigned to it an element of political science, as well as one of dialectic.

3 (R^2 133, R^3 139)

Ibid. 3. 1. 13. The most famous of Gorgias' disciples was Isocrates—although the authorities are not agreed on the question who Isocrates' teacher was; but we believe Aristotle.

[1] i.e. Xenophon.

SYMPOSIUM

TESTIMONIA

PLU. *Mor.* 612 d–e. To forget entirely what has been said and done in wine seems not only to conflict with the reputed tendency of the table to promote friendliness, but also to have the witness of the most famous philosophers against it—Plato, Xenophon, Aristotle, and Speusippus, Epicurus, Prytanis, Hieronymus, and Dion the Academic, who have thought it worth some trouble to record sayings made at the wine-table.

MACROB. *Sat.* 7. 3. 23. I advise you at your feasts . . . either to propound or yourselves to resolve questions suitable to the occasion. This kind of thing the ancients were so far from thinking ridiculous that both Aristotle and Plutarch and your Apuleius wrote on such questions.

1[1] (R² 175, R³ 100)

ATH. 178 e–f. Homer, exact in all things, did not omit even this small thing, that we ought to tend and wash our poor bodies before going to a meal. At least he says of Odysseus that before the feast at the Phaeacian court 'The housekeeper straightway bade him bathe'.[2] And of Telemachus' companions he says, 'They went to the polished baths and bathed'.[3] For it was unbecoming, as Aristotle says, to go to the drinking-party covered with sweat and dust; a man of taste, as Heraclitus says, should not be slovenly or unwashed or delight in mire.

[1] R³'s fr. 99 is omitted because, even if Nauck's emendation Ἀριστοτέλους is right, there is no reason for supposing the passage to refer to Aristotle's *Symposium*.

[2] *Od.* 8. 449

[3] *Od.* 4. 48.

2 (R² 08, R³ 101)

ATH. 674 e–675 a. Sappho bids those who do sacrifice to be crowned with chaplets, as being something gayer and more pleasing to the gods. And Aristotle in his *Symposium* says that we offer nothing mutilated to the gods, but things perfect and whole; now that which is complete is perfect, and garlanding oneself signifies a sort of completion. Homer says 'The young men crowned the bowls with wine',[1] and 'The god crowns his beauty with words';[2] those who are unshapely in aspect, he means, are made good by the charm of speech. This, then, is what the garland seems to mean. Accordingly on occasions of grief we arrange things in the opposite way; in fellow-feeling for the departed we disfigure ourselves by cutting our hair and giving up our garlands.

Cf. *Schol. in Theocr.* 3. 21.

3 (R² 98, R³ 102)

ATH. 40 c–d. Seleucus says it was the ancient custom not to take wine, beyond the ordinary, or to enjoy any other luxury, except in honour of the gods. It was for this reason that they used the words 'festivity', 'feast', and 'drunkenness'; the first because they thought it was in honour of the gods that we ought to drink wine, the second because it was in honour of the gods that they assembled and came together (this is what Homer's 'rich feast'[3] means), while drunkenness, Aristotle says, is so called because it is the taking of wine after sacrifices to the gods.[4]

PHILO, *De Plant.* 34. 141. What the lawgiver said about drunkenness we shall later see precisely; let us now examine[5] what others thought. The question was much debated by many of the philosophers, and is propounded thus: 'Will the wise man get drunk?' 'Getting drunk' has two meanings;

[1] *Il.* 1. 470. [2] *Od.* 8. 170. [3] *Od.* 3. 420, etc.

[4] The common element is the theta in θεός, θοινή, θαλία, θύειν, μεθύειν.

[5] Reading in R. 99. 13 ἐξερευνήσωμεν, with Cohn and Wendland.

in one it is equivalent to being in wine; in the other to being silly when in wine. Of those who attacked the problem, some said the wise man would neither drink too much strong drink nor become maudlin. . . . 35. 144. The others declared that being in wine was becoming even to a good man, while being maudlin was not. . . . 38. 154. Unmixed drink the ancients called not only wine but also liquor; at all events the name is often used in poetry, so that if synonyms ('wine' and 'liquor') are names for a single thing, words derived from them ('being in wine' and 'being in liquor') will differ only in sound[1]. . . . 155. If the good man is to be in wine, he will also get drunk. . . . 156. We have mentioned one argument to show that the wise man will get drunk; the second is as follows. . . . 39. 160. My purpose has been to show that people do not now take strong drink in the way the ancients did. . . . 161. Our fathers began every good work with sacred rites, thinking that so the result would be most propitious, because they had begun with prayer and sacrifice; and even if the need for action was urgent, still they waited, thinking that more haste is sometimes less speed. Speed without foresight was, they thought, harmful, while leisureliness with good hope for the future was advantageous. Knowing, then, that even[2] the enjoyment and use of wine needs much care, they did not take strong drink to their fill[3] nor at all times, but in fitting manner and in due season. They first prayed and offered sacrifices and propitiated the divine power, and purified their bodies and souls, the former with baths and the latter with the streams of laws and right education, and then turned, cheerful and rejoicing, to a relaxed way of life; they often did not return to their homes but continued[4] in the temples in which they had sacrificed, so that, remembering the sacrifices and respecting the place, they might feast in the manner most befitting to a sacred place, erring neither in word nor in action. It is from this, indeed, that

[1] Reading in R. 99. 23–24 *ἐμφερόμενον, ὥστ' εἰ τὰ συνωνυμοῦντα καθ' ἑνὸς ὑποκειμένου λέγεται, οἶνος καὶ μεθύ, καὶ τὰ ἀπὸ τούτων οὐδὲν ὅτι μὴ φωναῖς διοίσει μόνον, τό τε οἰνοῦσθαι καὶ τὸ μεθύειν* [*ἕν*], with Cohn and Wendland.

[2] Reading in R. 100. 8 *ὅτι καὶ ἡ*, with Cohn and Wendland.

[3] Reading in R. 100. 9 *ἄδην*, with Cohn and Wendland.

[4] Reading in R. 100. 16 *διατελοῦντες*, with Cohn and Wendland.

they say getting drunk gets its name, because it was the custom of our forefathers to take wine after sacrifice.[1] To whom, then, could the manner we have described of using strong drink be more fitting than to wise men, to whom[2] the sacrifice that precedes the drinking is also fitting? For one might almost say that no bad man really performs the sacred rites, even if without cessation he brings ten thousand oxen to the altar every day. For the most necessary sacrifice, his mind, is blemished, and it is not lawful for blemished persons to touch the altar. This is the second argument. . . . 40. 165–6. The third depends[3] on a different guess at the etymology. Some people think that drunkenness is so called not only because it is achieved after sacrifice, but also because it causes relaxation of soul.[4] Now when the reasoning of the foolish is relaxed, that leads to the strengthening of many errors, but when that of the wise is relaxed, it leads to the enjoyment of relaxation, contentment, and cheerfulness. For a wise man who has taken wine becomes sweeter-tempered than he was when sober, so that in this respect too[5] we should make no mistake in saying that he will get drunk.

Cf. Plu. *Mor.* 503 e–504 b.

4 (R^2 99, R^3 103)

Apollon. *Mirab.* 25 (Keller). Aristotle in his book on drunkenness says that Andron of Argos, though he ate many salty and dry foods, remained all through his life without thirst and without drink. Besides, he twice travelled to Ammon through the desert, eating dry barley-groats but taking no liquid.

Cf. Ath. 44 d, Diog. Laert. 9. 11. 81, Sext. Emp. *Pyrr.* 1. 84.

1 *μεθύειν = μετά + θύειν* !

2 Omitting *νῦν* in R. 100. 22, with Cohn and Wendland.

3 Reading in R. 100. 28–101. 2 *τρίτος . . . ἠρτημένος*, with Cohn and Wendland.

4 *μέθη–μέθεσις*.

5 Reading in R. 101. 8 *οὐδ' ἂν ταύτῃ*, with Cohn and Wendland.

5 (R^2 100, R^3 104)

ATH. 641 d–e. Aristotle in his book on drunkenness calls[1] these, as we do, second tables, in these words: 'We must consider that a sweetmeat differs entirely from food, as much as[2] an eatable differs from a "sucket" (the old Greek name for a sweetmeat when it is served as dessert);[3] so that the first person to speak of "second tables" seems to have been justified; for the eating of sweets is a sort of extra dinner, and a sweet course forms a second meal.'

Ibid. 641 b. Aristotle in his book on drunkenness says that sweetmeats were called by our ancestors suckets; they were a kind of extra dinner.

Cf. *Schol. in Aristoph. Pacem* 1. 772.

6 (R^2 218, R^3 105)

PS.-JUL. *Ep.* 391 b–c. The fig is not only pleasant to the taste, but also better for the digestion. It is so useful to mankind that Aristotle even calls it an antidote to every poison, and says it is just for that reason that at meals[4] it is served both as an hors-d'œuvre[5] and as dessert, as though it were being wrapped round the iniquities of the food in preference to any other sacred antidote. And indeed that the fig is dedicated to the gods, is placed on the altar in every sacrifice, and is a better incense than any frankincense, this is not my account only; anyone who has learned its use knows that this is the account any wise man skilled in sacred rites would give.

7 (R^2 101, R^3 106)

ATH. 447 a–b. As Aristotle says in his book on drunkenness, those who have drunk the barley liquor called beer fall on

[1] Reading in R. 102. 9 *προσαγορεύει*, with Kaibel.
[2] Reading in R. 102. 11 *ὅσον*, with the MSS.
[3] Omitting *τὰ βρώματα* in R. 102. 12 with Kaibel.
[4] Reading in R. 102. 26 *κἀν τοῖς δείπνοις*, with Hercher.
[5] Reading in R. 102. 27 *προπαρατίθεσθαι*, with Hercher.

their backs; he says: 'The liquor made from barley called beer has a certain peculiarity; people who are intoxicated by other liquors fall in all sorts of directions—to the left, to the right, on their faces, on their backs; only those who are intoxicated with beer always fall backwards and lie on their backs.'

Cf. ATH. 34 b.

8 (R^2 102, R^3 107)

ATH. 429 c–d. Aristotle in his book on drunkenness says: 'If the wine is boiled down to a moderate extent it is less intoxicating'; the force of the liquor, he says, is weakened by the boiling down. 'The old', he adds, 'are intoxicated most quickly, owing to the scarcity and weakness of the natural heat in them. But also those who are very young are intoxicated fairly quickly because of the abundance of the inherent heat; they are easily overcome by the added heat from the wine. Of dumb animals, too, pigs get intoxicated if they are fed with masses of pressed grapes; ravens and dogs if they eat the wine-plant; monkeys and elephants if they drink wine. This is why they capture monkeys and ravens by intoxicating the former with wine or the latter with wine-plant.'

9 (R^2 103, R^3 108)

PLU. *Mor.* 650 a. Florus was surprised at the fact that Aristotle, who has written in his book on drunkenness that old men are overtaken most easily, and women least easily, by drunkenness, did not work out the reason, a thing he was not wont to fail to do.

10 (R^2 104, R^3 109)

ATH. 429 f. The cup called Samagoreion made from three pints mixed will, according to Aristotle, intoxicate more than forty men.

11 (R² 105–6, R³ 110–11)

ATH. 464 c–d. Aristotle in his book on drunkenness says: 'The so-called Rhodian cups are introduced at drinking parties both because of the pleasure they give and because when they are heated they make the wine less intoxicating; they are made by boiling water in which myrrh and rushes and the like have been thrown, and when they are poured into the wine the drinkers get less intoxicated.' Elsewhere he says: 'The Rhodian cups are made of myrrh, rushes, dill,[1] saffron, balsam, cardamom, and cinnamon boiled together; the cup made from these[2], when poured into the wine, checks intoxication, so that it even restrains people from sexual intercourse, by cooling down their spirits.'

Cf. ibid. 496 f.

12

PLU. *Mor.* 651 f–652 a. 'I want to learn whence came our notion that wine is cold.' 'You think', said I, 'that that is our view?' 'Whose is it, then?' he said. 'Well, I remember,' said I, 'happening—not lately but quite a while ago—on a discussion of this problem by Aristotle.'

[1] Reading in R. 104. 19 *σχοίνου, ἀνήθου*, with Wilamowitz.
[2] Omitting *καί* in R. 104. 20, with the MSS.

SOPHISTES

1 (R^2 54, R^3 65)

DIOG. LAERT. 8. 2. 57 (3). Aristotle says in the *Sophistes* that Empedocles first discovered rhetoric, and Zeno dialectic.

Cf. ibid. 9. 5. 25 (4), and SEXT. EMP. *Dogm.* 1. 6–7.

2 (R^2 55, R^3 66)

DIOG. LAERT. 8. 2. 63 (9). Aristotle, too, says that Empedocles was free-minded and averse to all rule, since he declined the kingship which was offered him (as Xanthus says in his account of him)—no doubt because he preferred the simple life.

3 (R^2 56, R^3 67)

DIOG. LAERT. 9. 8. 54 (5). The first of his books that Protagoras read in public was that about the gods. . . . He read it at Athens, in the house of Euripides, or, as some say, in that of Heraclides, while others say it was in the Lyceum; his pupil Archagoras the son of Theodotus read it for him. He was accused by Pythodorus son of Polyzelus, one of the Four Hundred; though Aristotle says his accuser was Euathlus.

EUDEMUS, or ON SOUL

1 (R² 32, R³ 37, W 1)

Cic. *Div. ad Brut.* I. 25. 53. What? Is the great, the almost divine, intellect of Aristotle in error, or does he wish others to fall into error, when he writes that his friend Eudemus of Cyprus while on a journey to Macedonia came to Pherae, a Thessalian town of considerable note at the time, but held in cruel subjection by the tyrant Alexander. In that town Eudemus fell so ill that all the doctors feared for his life. He dreamed that a handsome young man told him that he would soon recover, that in a few days the tyrant Alexander would die, and that in the fifth year thereafter Eudemus himself would return home. Aristotle writes that the first two predictions were fulfilled forthwith; Eudemus recovered and the tyrant was killed by his wife's brothers. But towards the end of the fifth year, when the dream had led him to hope that he would return from Sicily to Cyprus, he died in battle at Syracuse. And so the dream had been interpreted as meaning that when Eudemus' soul had left his body, it had returned to its home.

Plu. *Dion* 22. 3. With Dion acted many of the politicians, and of the philosophers Eudemus the Cyprian, to whom after his death Aristotle dedicated his dialogue *On Soul*, and Timonides the Leucadian.

2 (R² 33, R³ 38, W 2)

Them. *in De An.* 106. 29–107. 5. Of the arguments that Plato used about the immortality of the soul, pretty much the greater number and the most weighty find their basis in the reason. This is true both of the argument from self-movement (for it was shown that only the reason is self-moved, if we take movement to mean activity), of that which assumes learning to be recollection, and of that which speaks of the soul's likeness to God. Of the other arguments those thought the more convincing could be without difficulty referred to the reason, and also the more convincing of those worked out by Aristotle himself in the *Eudemus*. From these facts it is clear that Plato, also, takes reason alone to be immortal.

3 (R^2 33, R^3 39, W 3)

ELIAS *in Cat.* 114. 25. Aristotle establishes the immortality of the soul in his acroamatic works[1] as well, and there he establishes it by conclusive arguments, but in the dialogues he naturally uses probable arguments. . . . 32. In his dialogues he says that the soul must be immortal because we all instinctively make libations to the departed and swear by the departed, but no one can make a libation to that which is completely non-existent, or swear by it. . . . 115. 11–12. It is chiefly in his dialogues that Aristotle seems to announce the immortality of the soul.

4 (R^2 34, R^3 40, W 4)

PROCL. *in Tim.* 338 c. Plato joined the soul to the body immediately, cutting out all the problems about the descent of the soul. . . . d. Nor will he tell us here what happens after the departure of the soul . . . because (as I will maintain) he confines himself to what is fitting to the purpose of the dialogue, and admits here just so much of the theory of the soul as is physical, describing the soul's companionship with the body. Aristotle in emulation of him treats physically of the soul in the *De Anima*, saying nothing either about its descent or about its fortunes; but in his dialogues he dealt separately with those matters and offered[2] the preceding argument.

5 (R^2 35, R^3 41, W 5)

PROCL. *in Remp.* 2. 349. 13–26 (Kroll). The divine Aristotle, also, states the reason why the soul on coming hither from

[1] i.e. scientific works representing Aristotle's teaching to the members of his school.

[2] Reading in R. 47. 1 κατεβάλετο, with Diehl.

yonder forgets the sights it saw there, but on going from here remembers yonder its experiences here. We must accept[1] the argument; for he himself says that on their journey from health to disease some people forget even the letters they had learned, but that no one ever has this experience when passing from disease to health; and that life without the body, being natural to souls, is like health, and life in the body, as being unnatural, is like disease. For there they live according to nature, but here contrary to nature; so that it naturally results[2] that souls that pass from yonder forget the things there, while souls that pass yonder from this world continue to remember the things in it.

6 (R² 40, R³ 44, W 6)

PLU. *Mor.* 115 b–e. Many wise men, as Crantor says, not only recently but long ago have bewailed the human lot, thinking life a punishment, and merely to be born a man the greatest of misfortunes. Aristotle says that even Silenus revealed this to Midas when caught by him. But it is better to record the philosopher's very words. He says this in the work called *Eudemus* or *On the Soul*: 'Wherefore, best and most blessed of all men, not only[3] do we think the dead happy and blessed, and think it impious[4] to say anything untrue about them and to slander them, since they have already become better and greater—this custom is so ancient and long established among us that absolutely no one knows either the time of its origin or who first established it; it seems to have been followed continuously for endless ages—not only that, but you see the saying that has been current in the mouths of men for many years.'[5] 'What is that?' said the other. And he said in answer: 'Why, that not to be born is best of all, and death better than life; to many a man has the heavenly voice so testified. This, they say, is what happened

[1] Reading in R. 47. 7 *ἀποδεκτέον*, with Kroll.

[2] Reading in R. 47. 12–13 *ὑγιείᾳ, τὴν δὲ ἐν σώμασιν, ὡς παρὰ φύσιν, νόσῳ. ζῆν γὰρ ἐκεῖ μὲν κατὰ φύσιν αὐτάς, ἐνταῦθα δὲ παρὰ φύσιν ὥστ' εἰκότως συμβαίνειν*, with Kroll.

[3] Omitting in R. 48. 11 *καί* before *πρός*, with one MS.

[4] Omitting *ἡγούμεθα* in R. 48. 14, with Bernays.

[5] Reading in R. 48. 20 (for *πάλαι*) *πολλῶν ἐτῶν*, with Paton.

to the famous Midas when he had caught Silenus and asked him what is the best thing for men and the thing most desirable of all; Silenus at first would not say anything but maintained unbroken silence; but when at last by using every device Midas had with difficulty induced him to say something, he said under compulsion:[1] "Shortlived seed of a toilsome spirit and of a hard fate, why do you force me to say what it is better for you not to know? The most painless life is that lived in ignorance of one's own ills. To men it is quite impossible for the best thing of all to happen, nor can they share in the nature of the best (for it is best for all men and women not to be born), but the next best, and the best achievable for men,[2] is, having been born, to die as soon as may be." It is clear that[3] by this he meant that the time spent in death is better than that spent in life.'

7 (R^2 41, R^3 45, W 7)

PHILOP. *in De An.* 141. 22. Aristotle, having blamed alike all those who had spoken of the soul, for having said nothing about the body which was to receive it. . . . 30 naturally goes on to link with this his opinion about the soul. Some thinkers looked to the same fact, that it is not a body of any chance constitution[4] that shares in soul, but it needs a definite constitution,[5] just as attunement is not produced by any chance state of the strings but needs[6] a definite degree of tension of them; they thought, therefore, that the soul too is an attunement of the body, and that the different kinds of soul answer to the[7] different attunements of the body. This opinion Aristotle states and refutes. At first he merely records the opinion itself, but presently he sets forth the arguments that led them to it. He had already opposed this opinion elsewhere, in the dialogue *Eudemus*, and before him Plato in the *Phaedo* had used some five arguments against this view. . . .

[1] Reading in R. 49. 2 ἀναγκαζόμενον, with Paton.
[2] Reading in R. 49. 8 ἀνθρώποις, with Wilamowitz.
[3] Reading in R. 49. 9–10 δῆλον οὖν ὅτι ὡς, with Reiske.
[4] Reading in R. 49. 17 ὡς ἔτυχεν ἔχον, with Hayduck.
[5] Reading in R. 49. 17–18 δεῖται τοιῆσδε κράσεως, with Hayduck.
[6] Reading in R. 49. 19 δεῖται, with Hayduck.
[7] Reading in R. 49. 20 τὰς διαφόρους, with Hayduck.

144. 21. These are Plato's five objections. Aristotle himself, as I have already said, has used in the dialogue *Eudemus* the two following objections. One goes thus: 'Attunement', he says, 'has a contrary, lack of attunement, but the soul has no contrary. Therefore the soul is not an attunement.' One might reply to this that there is strictly no contrary to attunement,[1] but rather[2] an indefinite privation, and the soul, as being a form, has an indefinite opposite, and as we say in the case of music that a certain kind of lack of attunement changes into attunement,[3] so a certain kind of privation changes into soul. Aristotle's second objection[4] is this: 'The contrary of the attunement of the body is the lack of attunement of the body, and the lack of attunement of the living body is disease, weakness, and ugliness; of which, disease is lack of attunement of the elements, weakness lack of attunement of the tissues, ugliness lack of attunement of the organs. If, then, lack of attunement is disease, weakness, and ugliness, attunement is health, strength, and beauty; but soul is none of these, neither health nor strength nor beauty; for even Thersites, the ugliest of men, had a soul. Therefore the soul is not an attunement.' This is what Aristotle says in the *Eudemus*. But here[5] he has used four objections to refute this opinion, of which the third is the second of those in the *Eudemus*. . . . 145. 21. Aristotle says 'in public discussions'. He must mean either his unwritten discussions with his associates or the exoteric writings (among which are the dialogues, e.g. the *Eudemus*), which are called exoteric because they were not written for his genuine disciples, but for the general advantage of the many. . . . 147. 6–10. 'It is more appropriate to call health (or generally the good state of the body) an attunement than to assert this of the soul.' This is the third objection (the second in the *Eudemus*). That health is an attunement he has shown in the *Eudemus* from its being the contrary of disease; we have stated above the course of the syllogism.

[1] Omitting in R. 50. 8 *ἐναντίον* after *κυρίως*, with Hayduck.
[2] Reading in R. 50. 9 *ἀλλὰ μᾶλλον στέρησις*, with Hayduck.
[3] Reading in R. 50. 11 *τοιάνδε ἀναρμοστίαν μεταβαίνειν εἰς τὴν ἁρμονίαν*, with Hayduck.
[4] Reading in R. 50. 12 *δεύτερον*, with Hayduck.
[5] i.e. in the *De Anima*.

SIMP. *in De An.* 53. 1–4. By the arguments used in public discussion Aristotle means those of the arguments used which are adapted to the intelligence of most people, hinting perhaps at those in the *Phaedo*, but meaning also those used by himself in the dialogue *Eudemus* to refute the attunement theory.

THEM. *in De An.* 24. 13. Another opinion about the soul has been handed down, which is as plausible as any, and has rendered account of itself and been examined both in public and in private discussions. Some people say soul is an attunement; for attunement is a mixture and combination of contraries, and the body is composed of contraries, so that that which brings these into concord and harmonizes them—hot and cold, moist and dry, hard and soft, and all the other contrarieties of the elements—is nothing other than soul, just as the attunement of notes blends low notes with high. The argument is plausible, but has been refuted in many places both by Aristotle and by Plato. The soul, they say, is prior to body, but harmony is posterior; the soul rules and oversees the body and often fights it, but harmony does not fight with the things that have been harmonized; harmony admits of more and less, soul does not; harmony, so long as it is preserved, does not admit disharmony, but soul admits wickedness; if the disharmony of the body is disease, ugliness, or weakness, the harmony of the body must be beauty, health, and strength, not soul—all these things have been said by the philosophers elsewhere; but what Aristotle says now is this. . . . 25. 23–25. That those who say the soul is a harmony would seem to be neither very near to nor very far from the truth is clear, then, both from what Aristotle has said now and from what he has said elsewhere.

OLYMP. *in Phd.* 173. 20 (Norvin). Aristotle in the *Eudemus* objects as follows: 'Disharmony is contrary to harmony, but soul has no contrary, since it is a substance; the conclusion is obvious. Again, if the disharmony of the elements of an animal is disease, their harmony must be health, not soul. . . . 30. The third argument is the same as the second in the *Eudemus*.

SOPHON. *in De An.* 25. 4–8. There has been handed down yet another opinion about the soul, which many people find plausible, as much so as any of those that are recorded. It has, however, already been brought to account and refuted by appropriate arguments which have been published—both by our arguments addressed to Eudemus and by those in Plato's *Phaedo*; but none the less they will be criticized now as well. Some say the soul is a harmony.

8 (R² 42, R³ 46, W 8)

SIMP. *in De An.* 221. 20–33. Plato is in every case accustomed to call by the same name the Forms and the things that are formed according to them. But Aristotle, when the thing formed is divisible, avoids using the same name, because of the great difference between the divisible thing and the indivisible form. The reasoning soul he describes not only as limited but also as a limit; for as it is between the indivisible and the divisible, being in a sense both, so too it is between the limit and the limited, exhibiting both characters—the latter as moving discursively, the former because it always moves in obedience to limits and because all that has been unfolded is gathered into one; in this respect it is likened to the limiting reason. And because of this he says in his dialogue on the soul called *Eudemus* that the soul is a form, and praises those who describe the soul as receptive of forms—not the whole soul but the rational soul, as knowing the forms that have the second degree of truth: for it is to reason, which is greater than soul, that the really true forms correspond.

9 (R² 38, R³ 43)

PLU. *Mor.* 733 c. Aristotle has recorded that in Cilicia Timon's grandmother hibernated two months in each year, giving no sign of life except by breathing.

10

PLU. *Mor.* 382 d–e. The knowledge of that which is knowable, pure, and simple, flashing like lightning through the soul, grants it at times to touch and see. This is why Plato and Aristotle call this part of philosophy a mystic vision, inasmuch as those who forsake these confused and various objects of opinion leap in thought to that primary, simple, and immaterial object, and, gaining true contact with the pure truth about it, think that, as though by initiation into the mysteries, they have attained the end of philosophy.

11

AL-KINDĪ, cod. Taimuriyye Falsafa 55. Aristotle tells of the Greek king whose soul was caught up in ecstasy, and who for many days remained neither alive nor dead. When he came to himself, he told the bystanders of various things in the invisible world, and related what he had seen—souls, forms, and angels; he gave the proofs of this by foretelling to all his acquaintances how long each of them would live. All he had said was put to the proof, and no one exceeded the span of life that he had assigned. He prophesied, too, that after a year a chasm would open in the country of Elis, and after two years a flood would occur in another place; and everything happened as he had said. Aristotle asserts that the reason of this was that his soul had acquired this knowledge just because it had been near to leaving his body and had been in a certain way separated from it, and so had seen what it had seen. How much greater marvels of the upper world of the kingdom would it have seen, then, if it had really left his body!

AL-KINDĪ, cod. Aya Sofia 4832, fol. 34. Aristotle asserts of the soul that it is a simple substance whose actions are manifested in bodies.

12

SERV. *in Aen.* 6. 448. 'Caeneus, now a woman.' Caenis was a girl who won from Neptune as the price of her shame a change of sex. . . . Virgil refers to the Platonic or Aristotelian view that souls often by metempsychosis change their sex.

NERINTHUS[1]

1 (R^2 53, R^3 64)

THEM. *Or.* 295 c–d. This man, after some slight association with my studies or amusements—whichever you call them—had almost the same experience as the philosopher Axiothea, Zeno of Citium, and the Corinthian farmer. Axiothea, after reading a book of Plato's *Republic*, migrated from Arcadia to Athens and attended Plato's lectures for a long time without being discovered to be a woman—like Lycomedes' Achilles. The Corinthian farmer after coming into contact with Gorgias—not Gorgias himself but the dialogue Plato wrote in criticism of the sophist—forthwith gave up his farm and his vines, put his soul under Plato's guidance, and made it a seed-bed and a planting ground for Plato's philosophy. This is the man whom Aristotle honours in his Corinthian dialogue. The facts about Zeno are well known and are recounted by many writers—that the *Apology* of Socrates brought him from Phoenicia to the painted Stoa.

[1] The work *Nerinthus,* which occurs in the lists of Aristotelian works preserved by Diogenes Laertius and Hesychius, is not mentioned under that name by any other ancient writer, nor does the name Nerinthus occur elsewhere. The identification of the work with the 'Corinthian dialogue' named by Themistius, and of Nerinthus with the 'Corinthian farmer', is purely conjectural, but not unlikely to be right.

EROTICUS[1]

1 (R^2 91, R^3 96)

Ath. 564 b. Aristotle says that lovers look at no other part of the body of their beloved than the eyes, in which modesty dwells.

2 (R^2 92, R^3 97)

Plu. *Pel.* 18. 4. It is said also that Iolaus, who was the beloved of Hercules, shares in the contests of the Thebans and throws the spear with them. Aristotle says that even in his time lovers and their beloved still pledged their troth on the tomb of Iolaus.

Cf. Plu. *Mor.* 761 d–e.

3 (R^2 93, R^3 98)

Plu. *Mor.* 760 e–761 b. 'You know, I suppose, what led to the death of Cleomachus of Pharsalus in battle. . . . He came with the Thessalian army as an ally to the people of Chalcis, when their war with the Eretrians was at its height. The Chalcidians thought their infantry strong, but the repulsing of the enemy's cavalry was a formidable task; so his allies called on Cleomachus, whose courage was famous, to lead the attack against the cavalry. He asked his beloved, who was present, whether he was going to watch the contest. When the young man said "Yes", greeted him lovingly, and nodded consent, Cleomachus, emboldened by this, called the best of the Thessalians together round him, made a brilliant charge, and fell on the enemy with such vigour as to throw the cavalry into confusion and rout them. When as a result

[1] R^2's fr. 95 is omitted, because ἐν δευτέρῳ ἐρωτικῶν seems to refer not to the *Eroticus*, which both Diogenes Laertius and Hesychius describe as having one book, but to the *θέσεις ἐρωτικαί*, which they both describe as having four books.

of this the hoplites also took to flight, the Chalcidians gained a mighty victory; but it so happened that Cleomachus was killed. The Chalcidians show in their market-place his tomb, on which to this day the great pillar stands; and to the love of boys, which formerly they had reprehended, they from that time gave more devotion and honour than others do. Aristotle, however, says that Cleomachus died in other fashion after defeating the Eretrians in battle, that the lover in question was a Chalcidian from Thrace who was sent to help the Chalcidians in Euboea, and that this is the origin of the Chalcidian song "Children, heirs of Graces and of splendid fathers, grudge not to the good the company of youthful prime; for along with courage limb-loosing love flourishes in the cities of the Chalcidians".'

4

AL-DAILAMI, cod. Tübingen Weisweiler 81. It is said in a certain book of the ancients that the pupils of Aristotle assembled before him one day. And Aristotle said to them: 'While I was standing on a hill I saw a youth, who stood on a terrace roof and recited a poem, the meaning of which was: Whoever dies of passionate love, let him die in this manner; there is no good in love without death.' Then said his pupil Issos: 'O philosopher, inform us concerning the essence of love.' And Aristotle replied: 'Love is an impulse which is generated in the heart; when it is once generated, it moves and grows; afterwards it becomes mature. When it has become mature it is joined by affections of appetite whenever the lover in the depth of his heart increases in his excitement, his perseverance, his desire, his concentrations, and his wishes. And that brings him to cupidity and urges him to demands, until it brings him to disquieting grief, continuous sleeplessness, and hopeless passion and sadness and destruction of mind.'

PROTREPTICUS

TESTIMONIA

Hist. Aug. 2. 97. 20–22 (Hohl). Nor, I suppose, are the arguments unknown which Cicero used in his *Hortensius*, which he modelled on the *Protrepticus*.

NONIUS 394. 26–28. (Lindsay), s.v. *contendere, intendere*. Cicero in the *Hortensius*: 'for great mental effort must be applied to the explaining of Aristotle, if you are to read him.'

MART. Cap. 5. 44. The question whether we ought to philosophize is discussed in the *Hortensius*.

1 (R^2 47, R^3 50, W 1)

STOB. 4. 32. 21. From Teles' *Epitome*. Zeno said that Crates, as he sat in a shoemaker's workshop, read aloud the *Protrepticus*, which Aristotle had written to Themison king of Cyprus, saying that no one had greater advantages for becoming a philosopher; he had great wealth, so that he could afford to spend money on philosophy, and had reputation as well. As he read, the shoemaker listened while he went on with his stitching, and Crates said: 'I think, Philiscus, that I shall inscribe a *Protrepticus* to you; for I see you have more advantages for the study of philosophy than were his[1] for whom Aristotle wrote.'

2 (R^2 50, R^3 51, W 2)

ALEX. APH. *in Top.* 149. 9–17. There are cases where, whichever interpretation we adopt, we can on the basis of it refute the proposition proposed. Suppose someone said we ought not to pursue philosophy. Then, since even to inquire whether we ought to philosophize or not is (as Aristotle himself said in the *Protrepticus*) to philosophize, and since to pursue

[1] Reading in R. 56. 21 ἢ ᾧ, with Diels.

philosophical insight is also to philosophize, by showing that each of these two things is natural to man we shall on all counts refute the proposition proposed. In this case[1] our proposition can be proved on both counts, but in the examples first quoted it cannot be proved on all counts or on each of two, but only on one or more.[2]

Cf. *Schol. in An. Pr.*, cod. Paris. 2064, f. 263 *a*, and Olymp. *in Alc.* p. 144 (Creuzer).

ELIAS *in Porph.* 3. 17–23. We may also reason as Aristotle does in his *Protrepticus*, in which he encourages young men to philosophize. He says this: 'If we ought to philosophize we ought to philosophize, and if we ought not to philosophize we ought to philosophize; in either case, therefore, we ought to philosophize. For[3] if philosophy exists we ought certainly to philosophize, because philosophy exists; and if it does not exist, even so we ought to examine why it does not exist, and in examining this we shall be philosophizing, because examination is what makes philosophy.'

DAVID, *Proll.* 9. 2–12. Aristotle, too, in a hortatory work in which he encourages young men to study philosophy, says that whether we ought or ought not to philosophize, we ought to philosophize, so that in either case we ought to philosophize. That is, if someone says philosophy does not exist, he will have used arguments destructive of philosophy, but if he has used arguments he is clearly philosophizing (for philosophy is the mother of arguments). But if he says philosophy exists, he again philosophizes; for he will have used arguments to prove that philosophy exists. In either case, then, they philosophize, both he who denies and he who does not deny that philosophy exists; for each has used arguments to justify what he says, and if he uses arguments

[1] Reading in R. 57. 4 *τούτου*, with Wallies.

[2] Reading in R. 57. 6 *οὐκ ἐκ πάντων ἢ ἑκατέρου ἀλλ' ἢ ἐκ τινὸς ἢ ἐκ τινῶν*, with Wallies.

[3] Omitting *τουτέστιν* in R. 57. 21, with Busse.

he clearly philosophizes; for philosophy is the mother of arguments.

Cf. LACT. *Inst.* 3. 16, and CLEM. AL. *Strom.* 6. 18, 162. 5.

3 (R² 89, R³ 57, W 3)

PAP. OXYRRH. 666 = STOB. 3. 3. 25. Seeing the misfortune of these men, we ought to avoid it and to consider[1] that happiness depends not on having many possessions but on the condition of the soul. For one would say that it is not the body which is decked with splendid clothing that is happy, but that which is healthy and in good condition, even if it has none of these things; and in the same way, if the soul has been disciplined, such a soul and such a man are to be called happy, not a man splendidly decked with outer things but himself worthless. It is not the horse which has a golden bit and costly harness, but is itself a poor creature, that we think worth anything; what we praise is the horse that is in good condition. Besides, when worthless men get abundant possessions, they come to value these more than the good of the soul; which is the basest of all conditions. If a man were inferior to his own servants, he would become contemptible; so too those for whom possessions are more important than their own nature must be considered miserable. This is indeed so; surfeit, as the proverb says, breeds insolence; possessions without discipline breed folly. For to those who are ill-disposed in soul neither wealth nor strength nor beauty is a good; the more lavishly one is endowed with these conditions, the more grievously and the more often do they hurt him who possesses them but has not wisdom. 'Give not a sword to a boy' means 'do not entrust riches to bad men'. All men would admit that wisdom comes from learning and from seeking the things to which philosophy gives the key; surely, then, we should sincerely pursue philosophy.

4 (W 4)

IAMBL. *Protr.* b. 37. 3–22. The things with which we are furnished for life—the body and bodily things—are provided

[1] Reading in R. 67. 4 δεῖ τὴν τούτων θεωροῦντας ἀτυχίαν φεύγειν καὶ νομίζειν, with Wilamowitz.

as tools, and the use of them is dangerous; they have rather the contrary effect, for those who do not use them fittingly. We ought therefore to desire knowledge—to acquire it and to use it aright—if we are to attain all these good results. We must, therefore, philosophize if we are to be good citizens, and to lead our own life usefully. Further, there are some branches of knowledge that produce each of the advantages in life, others that use this first kind, others that minister to them, others that commend them to our obedience; and in these last, as being more authoritative, consists the true good. If, then, only the science that has correctness of judgement, that which uses reason, that which envisages good as a whole—which is philosophy—can use and commend all things according to nature, we ought to philosophize in every possible way, since philosophy alone comprises right judgement and impeccable commanding wisdom.

5 (R³ 52, W 5)

IAMBL. *Comm. Math.* 26 (79. 1–81. 7 Festa). There have been some ancients and some moderns who have maintained the contrary view about mathematics, condemning it as completely useless and as contributing nothing to human life. Some people attack mathematics thus: 'If the end for whose sake philosophers say we ought to study it is useless, much more must the study itself be vain. Now about the end all who are thought to have attained the greatest precision in mathematics are pretty much agreed. Some say the end is the knowledge of injustice and justice, of evil and good, which they think akin to geometry and the kindred sciences; others think the end is wisdom with regard to nature and the like—the kind of wisdom introduced by the schools of Anaxagoras and Parmenides. He who is to consider these matters must therefore not fail to observe that all things good and useful for human life depend on use and action, not on mere knowledge. We become healthy not by knowing the things that produce health but by applying them to our bodies; we become wealthy not by knowing wealth but by possessing much substance; most important of all, we live well not by knowing something but by doing well; for this is true well-being. It follows that philosophy too, if it is to be profitable, must be either a doing of good things or useful as a means to such acts. Now, that neither philosophy nor any other of the aforesaid sciences is a doing of actions is clear to all; that it is not useful as a means to action can be seen from what follows. We have the best example in the difference between the sciences akin to philosophy and the doctrines that come under them. Take the things that geometers study by way of demonstration; we do not see them capable of doing any of these things. Land-surveyors can divide an estate, they can by virtue of experience deal with all the other properties of areas and regions; but those who concern themselves with mathematical proofs know how they ought to act, but cannot act. The same is true of music and of all the other arts in which the rôle of knowledge is distinct from that of experience. For those who have studied the proofs and syllogisms about harmony and such-like matters are (like the philosophers) accustomed to speculation but take no part in practice; if perchance they *can* handle any of these matters practically, when they have learned the proofs they at once, as if on purpose, do their jobs worse. On the other hand, those who do not know the theories, but have become habituated by training and hold sound opinions, are altogether superior for practical purposes. So too with regard to astronomical subjects—the sun, the moon, and the other stars—those who have studied the theoretical explanations know nothing that is useful to mankind, while those who have what these others call the navigational sciences can foretell for us storms, winds, and many other phenomena. Thus such sciences will be completely useless for practical purposes, and if they fall short of correct practice the love of learning misses the greatest goods.'

To these objections we reply that there are mathematical sciences and that they are capable of being acquired.

IAMBL. *Protr.* 6 (37. 26–41. 5 Pistelli). That we are capable of acquiring the sciences that deal with the just and the expedient, and also those that deal with nature and the rest of reality, it is easy to show. The prior is always more knowable than the posterior, and that which is naturally better more knowable than that which is worse. For knowledge is more concerned with things that are defined and ordered than with their contraries,[1] and more with causes than with effects; now good things are more defined and ordered than evil things, just as a good man is more defined and ordered than a bad man; there must be the same difference. Besides, things that are prior are causes, more than things that are posterior; for if the former are removed the things that have their being from them are removed, lines if numbers are removed, planes if lines are removed, solids if planes are removed, so-called 'syllables' if the letters are removed.[2] Therefore if soul is better than body (being more of the nature of a first principle), and there are arts and branches of knowledge concerned with the body, namely medicine and gymnastic (for we reckon these as sciences and say that some people possess them), clearly with regard to the soul too and its virtues there is a care and an art, and we can acquire these, since we can do this even with regard to things of which our ignorance is greater and knowledge is harder to come by. So too with regard to nature; it is far more necessary to have knowledge of the causes and the elements than to have knowledge of what follows from them; for the latter are not among the highest objects, and the first principles do not arise from them, but from and through the first principles all other things manifestly proceed and are constituted. Whether it be fire or air or number or other natures that are the causes and originals of other things, if we are ignorant of them we cannot know any of the other things. How could one recognize speech if one did not know the syllables, or know these if we knew none of the letters?

On the theme that there is knowledge of truth and of excellence of soul, and that we can acquire these, let this suffice. That it is the greatest of goods and the most valuable

[1] Reading in R. 60. 22 *ἐστιν ἢ τῶν ἐναντίων, ἔτι,* with Pistelli.

[2] Reading in R. 61. 1 (after *ἐπιπέδων*) *στοιχείων δὲ αἱ ὀνομαζόμεναι συλλαβαί,* with Wilpert.

of all things will be clear from what follows. We all agree that the best man and the man of strongest character ought to rule, and that the law alone is ruler and supreme; now the law is a form of wisdom, a form of words proceeding from wisdom. Again, what standard, what determinant, of what is good have we, other than the man of practical wisdom? The things that such a man would choose if his choice followed his knowledge are good, and their contraries evil. Now since all men choose by preference what accords with their own characters, the just man choosing to live justly, the brave man to live bravely, the temperate man to live temperately, similarly it is clear that the wise man will choose above all things to think wisely, that being the exercise of this faculty. It is clear, then, that according to the most authoritative opinion wisdom is the greatest of goods. We ought, therefore, not to flee philosophy, if it is, as we think, the acquisition and use of wisdom, and wisdom is among the greatest goods; and if in pursuit of gain we run many risks by sailing to the pillars of Hercules, we should not[1] shrink from labour or expense in the pursuit of wisdom. Indeed, it is the part of a slave to desire life rather than the good life, to follow the opinions of the many instead of expecting the many to follow one's own, to seek gain and pay no heed whatever to what is noble.

About the value and the greatness of the thing I think we have proved our case. That the acquisition of wisdom is much easier than that of other goods, one might be convinced by the following argument. Those who pursue philosophy get no reward from men to spur them to the efforts they make; they may have spent much on other branches of knowledge, yet in a short time their progress in philosophy outstrips their progress in other branches: that seems to me a sign of the easiness of philosophy. So too the fact that all men feel at home in philosophy and wish to spend their lives in the pursuit of it, leaving all other cares, is no small evidence that devotion[2] to it is pleasant; for no one is willing to suffer pain for long. Besides, the practice of philosophy is

[1] Reading in R. 62. 9 οὐδὲ δεῖ, with Pistelli.
[2] Reading in R. 63. 6 προσεδρεία, with Pistelli.

pre-eminent in that its followers need no tools or places for their work; wherever in the whole world one sets one's thought to work, it is surrounded on all sides by the presence of truth.

Thus it has been proved that philosophy is possible, that it is the greatest of goods, and that it is easy to acquire, so that on all counts it is fitting that we should eagerly lay hold of it.

PROCL. *in Eucl.* 28. 13–22 (Friedlein). That to those who pursue it mathematics is desirable for its own sake is shown, as Aristotle somewhere says, by the fact that, though no reward is held out to those who pursue it, facility in the study of mathematics increases so rapidly, and also by the fact that all who have had even a slight experience of what it can give one feel at home in it and are willing to spend their time in it, neglecting all else, so that those who despise the knowledge[1] of mathematics can never themselves have tasted its delights.

6 (W 6)

IAMBL. *Protr.* 7 (41. 15–43. 25 Pistelli). Part of us is soul, part body; the one rules, the other is ruled; the one uses, the other is present as its instrument. Therefore the use of the subject, i.e. of the instrument, is always directed to that which rules and uses. In the soul, reason is that which naturally rules and judges of our own interest; the other element follows and its nature is to be ruled. It is in accordance with its proper excellence that everything is well arranged; for to attain this excellence is a good. Further, when the chief parts, the supreme and most honourable parts, possess their proper excellence, then is a thing well arranged; therefore the natural excellence of that which is naturally better is the better. Now that which is by nature more originative and authoritative is the better, as man is in relation to the other animals; therefore soul is better than body (being more authoritative), and of soul, that which has reason and

[1] Reading in R. 63. 8 γνώσεως, with the MSS.

thought; for such is that which commands and forbids, and says what we ought to do or not to do. Whatever excellence, then, is the excellence of this part must be, for all beings in general and for us in particular, the most desirable of all things; for one would (methinks) maintain that this part is, either alone or above all other things, ourselves. Further, when a thing achieves in the best way that which is, not by accident but by its own nature, its work, then that thing must be said to be good, and that excellence in virtue of which each thing can achieve this result must be termed its supreme excellence. Now that which is composite and divisible into parts has several different activities, but that which is by nature simple and whose being does not consist in a relation to something else must have only one proper excellence. If then man is a simple animal and his being is ordered according to reason and intelligence, he has no function other than the attainment of the most exact truth, truth about reality; but if he is composed of several faculties, it is clear that where a thing naturally produces several results the best of them is always its proper work; health is the work of the doctor, and safety that of the steersman. Now we can name no better work of thought, or of the thinking part of the soul, than the attainment of truth. Truth therefore is the supreme work of this part of the soul. Now this work it does simply in virtue of knowledge, or rather in virtue of what is more completely knowledge, and the supreme end of this is contemplation. For when of two things one is worthy of choice for the sake of the other, the latter is better and more worthy of choice, e.g. pleasure than pleasant things, health than wholesome things; for these are said to be productive of those. Now than thought, which we maintain to be the faculty of the supreme element in us, there is nothing more worthy of choice, when one state is compared with another; for the part that knows, whether taken alone or in combination with other parts, is better than all the rest of the soul, and its excellence is knowledge. Therefore none of the particular excellences is its work; for it is better than all of them, and the end produced is always better than the knowledge that produces it. Nor is every excellence of the soul the work of wisdom in this way, nor is happiness. For if an excellence is to be productive, it will produce results different from itself; e.g. the art of building produces a house but is not part of a house; but wisdom is a part of excellence and of happiness; for we say that happiness either comes from wisdom or is it. According to this argument also, then, knowledge cannot be productive; for the end must be better than that which is coming to attain it, but nothing is better[1] than wisdom, unless it be one of the things we have named; but none of these is a product distinct from wisdom. Therefore we must say that this form of knowledge is contemplative, since that which is the end cannot be a process of production. Thinking and contemplation, therefore, are the work of virtue, and this is of all things the most worthy of choice for men, as (methinks) sight is for eyes; one would choose to have sight even if nothing other than sight itself were to result from it.

7 (W 7)

IAMBL. *Protr.* 7 (43. 25–45. 3 Pistelli). Further, if we love sight for its own sake, that is sufficient evidence that all men love thinking and knowing most of all. Again, if we love one thing because some property attends on it, clearly we shall wish more for that to which this property belongs in greater degree; e.g. if a man happens to choose walking because it is healthy, but running is more healthy for him and he can get it, he will (if he knows this) prefer running and choose it rather than walking. If, therefore, true opinion is like knowledge, then—since true opinion is worthy of choice in respect of being,[2] and in so far as it is, like knowledge by reason of being true—if knowledge is more true, it is more worthy of choice than true opinion. But living is distinguished from not living by sense-perception; it is by the presence and power of this that life has its distinctive character; if this is taken away life is not worth living—it is as though life itself were extinguished by the loss of sense-perception. Now of

[1] Reading βέλτιόν ἐστι, suggested by Pistelli.
[2] Reading ταύτῃ, suggested by Vitelli.

sense-perception one kind—the power of sight—is distinguished by being the clearest, and it is for this reason that we prefer it to the other senses; but every sense acquires knowledge by means of the body, as hearing perceives sound by means of the ears. Therefore if life is worthy of choice for the sake of perception, and perception is a kind of knowing, and we choose it because the soul can come to know by means of it, and (as we said before) of two things[1] that is always preferable which possesses the desirable quality more fully, then of the senses sight must be the most worthy of choice and honourable; but knowledge is preferable to it and to all the other senses, and to life itself, since it has a stronger grasp of truth;[2] so that all men aim at knowing, most of all things. For in loving life they love thinking and knowing; they value life for no other reason than for the sake of perception, and above all for the sake of sight; they evidently love this faculty in the highest degree because it is, in comparison with the other senses, simply a kind of knowledge.

8 (R² 1, R³ 53, W 8)

CIC. *Tusc.* 3. 28. 69. Therefore Aristotle, criticizing the old philosophers who had thought philosophy completed by their intellectual labours, says they were either very stupid or very conceited, but that he sees that, since great progress has been made in a few years, philosophy will in a short time be brought to completion.

IAMBL. *Comm. Math.* 26 (83. 6–22 Festa). The study of precision with regard to the truth is admittedly the youngest of all pursuits. For after the catastrophe of the flood men were compelled to think first about food and the preservation of life; when they had become better provided they worked out the arts that conduce to pleasure—music and the like; and it was only when they had acquired more than enough of the necessities of life that they essayed philosophy. But

[1] Reading ὅτι δυοῖν, with Jaeger.
[2] Reading κυριωτέρα ⟨οὖσα⟩, with Jaeger.

those who concern themselves with geometry and calculation and the other sciences have from small beginnings made by now such progress in a very short time as no other race has made in any of the arts. Yet while all men join in promoting the other arts by giving them public honour and rewarding the artists, we not only do not encourage mathematicians, but often even put difficulties in their way; yet these studies make most advance,[1] because they have a natural precedence; for that which is later in coming to be is prior in essence and perfection.

9 (R³ 55, W 9)

IAMBL. *Protr.* 8 (45. 4–47. 4 Pistelli). It is worth while to point out that the view in question follows from common opinions, from views that are clearly held by all men.

To everyone this much is plain, that no one would choose to live in receipt of the greatest wealth and power from men but deprived of thought and mad—not even if one were to be pursuing[2] with delight the most violent pleasures, as some madmen do. All men, then, it seems, shun above all things the loss of their wits. Now the contrary of witlessness is wisdom; and of two contraries one is to be avoided, the other to be chosen; as illness is to be avoided, so health is to be chosen. Thus according to this argument, too, in the light of common opinion, it seems that wisdom is most of all to be chosen, not for the sake of any[3] of its consequences. For even if a man had everything, but were destroyed and diseased in his thinking part, his life would not be worth living, since even the other good things could not profit him. Therefore all men, in so far as they are conscious of thinking and can taste its savour,[4] reckon other things as nothing, and for this reason not one of us would endure being drunk or a child throughout his life. For this reason too, though sleep is a very pleasant thing, it is not a thing to choose even if

[1] Reading in R. 64. 12 πλεῖστον, with Festa.

[2] Reading in R. 65. 7 διώκειν for ζώειν, with Diels.

[3] Reading in R. 65. 13–14 οὐ δι' ἕτερόν τι, with the MSS.

[4] Reading in R. 65. 18–19 αἰσθάνονται τοῦ φρονεῖν καὶ γεύεσθαι δύνανται τούτου τοῦ πράγματος, οὐδὲν οἴονται, with the MSS.

we suppose the sleeper to have all possible pleasures, because the images of sleep are false, while those of waking life are true. Sleep and waking differ in nothing but the fact that the soul when awake often knows the truth, but in sleep is always deceived; for the whole nature of dreams is an image and a lie.

Again, the shrinking of most men from death shows the soul's love of learning. For it shrinks from what it does not know, from darkness and obscurity, and naturally seeks what is manifest and knowable. This is, above all, the reason why we say we ought to honour and revere supremely, as authors of our greatest goods, the authors of our seeing the sun and the light—our fathers and mothers; these are, it seems, the authors of our thinking and seeing. It is for the same reason that we delight in things and men that are familiar, and call dear those whom we know. These things, then, show plainly that that which is knowable, manifest, and clear is a thing to be loved,[1] and if that which is knowable and clear, then also knowledge and thought are equally necessary to us.

Besides this, just as in the case of property it is not the same possession that conduces to life and to happy life, so too in the case of thought we do not, methinks, need the same with a view to mere life and with a view to the good life. The bulk of mankind may well be pardoned for doing as they do; while they pray for happiness they are content if they can but live. But unless one thinks one ought to endure living on any terms whatever, it is ridiculous not to endure every labour[2] and bestow every care to gain the wisdom which will know the truth.

10 *a* (R^2 49, R^3 59, W 10 *a*)

Iambl. *Protr.* 8 (47. 5–21 Pistelli). One might know this even from the following facts, if one viewed human life in a clear light. For one will find that all the things men think great are mere scene-painting; whence it is rightly said that man

[1] Reading in R. 66. 9 τὸ φανερὸν καὶ τὸ δῆλον ἀγαπητόν, with the MSS.
[2] Reading in R. 66. 18 πόνον ὑπομένειν, with the MSS.

is nothing, and nothing human is stable. Strength, size, beauty are a laugh and nothing more, and beauty[1] seems to be beauty only because we see nothing accurately. If one could have seen as clearly as they say Lynceus did, who saw through walls and trees, would one ever have thought any man endurable to look at, when one saw[2] of what poor materials he is made? Honours and reputation, these much envied things, are, even more than other things, full of indescribable folly; for to him who catches a glimpse of things eternal it seems foolish to busy himself with these things. What is there among human things that is long-lived or lasting? It is owing to our weakness, methinks, and the shortness of our life that even this appears great.

BOETH. *Consol.* 3. 8. How slight, how fragile is the tenure of those who boast of bodily goods! Can you surpass the elephant in size, the bull in strength, the tiger in speed? Look to the vastness, the durability, the speed of the heavens, and cease to marvel at those cheap possessions. No less than for these qualities, the heavens are admirable for the reason by which they are ruled. As for beauty, how swift is its passing—more fleeting than the flowers of spring! If, as Aristotle says, men had had the eyes of Lynceus, so that their sight could pierce through obstacles, would not the body of Alcibiades, so fair on the surface, have seemed most foul when its inward parts were seen? So it is not your own nature, but the weakness of the eyes which see you, that makes you seem beautiful. But consider how excessive is your desire of bodily goods, when you know that that which you admire can be dissolved by the paltry fire of a tertian fever.

CIC. *Tusc.* I. 39. 94. But what age can truly be called old? What possession of man is lasting? . . . Because we have nothing more, we call this lasting; all these things are called long or short according to the proportion of each that is given to each of us. By the river Hypanis, which flows into

[1] Reading in R. 70. 6 *κάλλος τε*, with the MSS.
[2] Reading in R. 70. 9 *ὁρῶν*, with the MSS.

the Pontus from the direction of Europe, Aristotle says there are born little creatures which live for but one day. One of these that has died at the eighth hour has died at an advanced age; one that has died at sunset is decrepit, especially if it is on a midsummer day. Compare our longest life with eternity; we shall be found as short-lived as these little creatures.

SEN. *Brev. Vit.* 1. 2. Aristotle's quarrel with the nature of things is most unsuitable to a wise man. He says that nature has indulged the animals so much that they live for five of our generations, while man, born to so many and such great achievements, has so much nearer a limit fixed for him.

10 *b* (R^2 36, R^3 60, W 10 *b*)

IAMB. *Protr.* 8 (47. 21–48. 9 Pistelli). Which of us, looking to these facts, would think himself happy and blessed—which of us, all of whom (in the first place) are from the start (as they say in the initiation rites) born as though for punishment? For it is an inspired saying of the ancients that the soul pays penalty and that we live for the punishment of great sins. The conjunction of the soul with the body looks very much like this. For as the Etruscans are said often to torture captives by chaining dead bodies face to face with the living, fitting part to part, so the soul seems to be extended throughout and affixed to all the sensitive members of the body.

AUG. *C. Iul. Pel.* 4. 15. 78. How much better and nearer the truth than yours were the views about the generation of men held by those whom Cicero, as though led and compelled by the very evidence of the facts, commemorates in the last part of the dialogue *Hortensius*! After mentioning the many facts we see and lament with regard to the vanity and the unhappiness[1] of men, he says: 'From which errors and cares of human life it results that sometimes those ancients—whether they were prophets or interpreters of the divine

[1] Reading in R. 71. 16 *infelicitate*, with Migne.

mind by the transmission of sacred rites—who said that we are born to expiate sins committed in a former life, seem to have had a glimpse of the truth, and that that is true which Aristotle says, that we are punished much as those were who once upon a time, when they had fallen into the hands of Etruscan robbers, were killed with studied cruelty; their bodies, the living with the dead, were bound as exactly[1] as possible one against another: so our minds, bound together with our bodies, are like the living joined with the dead.

Cf. CLEM. AL. *Protr.* I. 7. 4.

10 *c* (R² 48, R³ 61, W 10 *c*)

IAMBL. *Protr.* 8 (48. 9–21 Pistelli). Mankind has nothing worthy of consideration as being divine or blessed, except what there is in us of reason and wisdom; this alone of our possessions seems to be immortal, this alone to be divine. By virtue of being able to share in this faculty, life, however wretched and difficult by nature, is yet so cleverly arranged that man seems a god in comparison with all other creatures. For 'reason is the god in us' (whether it was Hermotimus or Anaxagoras that said so), and 'mortal life contains a portion of some god'. We ought, therefore, either to pursue philosophy or to say farewell to life and depart hence, since all other things seem to be great nonsense and folly.

CIC. *Fin.* 2. 13. 39–40. I shall hold that we must first exclude the opinions of Aristippus and the whole Cyrenaic school, who were not afraid to place the supreme good in the pleasure which moves our senses most delightfully, and spurned the freedom from pain of which you speak. They did not see that as the horse is born to run, the ox to plough, the dog to follow a scent, so man (as Aristotle says) is born as a sort of mortal god to do two things—for understanding and for action.

AUG. *Trin.* 14. 19. 26. Commending this contemplative wisdom . . . Cicero says at the end of the dialogue *Hortensius*:

[1] Reading in R. 71. 25 *aptissime*, with the MSS.

'To us . . . who spend our lives in philosophy this is a great hope—that if that by which we feel and think is mortal and perishable, we shall have a happy setting . . . and a rest from life; if, on the other hand, as the ancient, the greatest and far the most famous, philosophers thought, we have minds eternal and divine, then we should reflect that the more these minds have been constant in their courses—in the use of reason and in the desire of discovery—and the less they have mixed and implicated themselves in the vices and errors of mankind, the easier will be their ascent and return to heaven.' Then, adding this very clause and summing up his argument, he says: 'Wherefore—to bring my speech at last to an end—if we wish either to be quietly extinguished when we have lived our life in this prison, or to move without delay from this to a far better home, all our interest and concern must be bestowed on these studies.'

11 (W 11)

IAMBL. *Protr.* 9 (49. 3–52. 16 Pistelli). Of things that come into being some come from thought and art, e.g. a house or a ship (for the cause of both of these is a certain art and process of thought), while others come into being through no art, but by nature; nature is the cause of animals and plants, and all such things come into being according to nature. But some things, also, come into being as a result of chance; for of most of the things that come into being neither by art nor by nature nor of necessity, we say that they come into being by chance. Now of the things that come into being by chance none comes into being for the sake of anything, nor have they an end; but in the case of things that come into being by art there is an end and an object of purpose (for he who possesses the art will tell you the reason why he wrote, and for what purpose he did so), and this is better than that which comes into being for its sake. I speak of the things of which art is the cause by its own nature and not by accident; for we should describe the art of medicine as properly the art of health and not of disease, and architecture as the art of making houses, not of pulling them down.

Everything, therefore, that is according to art comes into being for the sake of something, and this is its best end, but that which comes into being by chance does not come into being for the sake of anything; something good might come into being by chance, yet in respect of chance and in so far as it results from chance it is not good—that which comes into being by chance is always indeterminate. But that which comes into being according to nature does so for an end, and is always constituted to better purpose than the product of art; for nature does not imitate art, but *vice versa*; art exists to aid nature and to fill up its deficiencies. For some things nature seems able to complete by itself without assistance, but others it does with difficulty or cannot do at all—in the matter of birth, to take an obvious example; some seeds generate without protection, whatever ground they fall into, others need the art of farming as well; and similarly some animals attain their full nature by themselves, but man needs many arts for his preservation, both at birth and in the matter of nutrition later. If, then, art imitates nature, it is from nature that the arts have derived the characteristic that all their products come into being for an end; for we should describe as coming into being for an end everything that comes into being rightly. Now that which comes into being beautifully comes into being rightly; and everything that comes into being or has come into being according to nature[1] comes into or has come into being beautifully, since that which is contrary to nature is bad and contrary to that which is according to nature; natural coming into being,[2] therefore, is for an end. This one can see from any one of our parts; if you were to consider the eyelid, you would see that it has come into being not at random but to aid the eyes—to give them rest and to ward off things that are falling on to them. Therefore that for the sake of which something has come into being is the same as that for which it ought to have come into being; if it was right that a ship should come into being to provide transport by sea, it is for that reason that it has come into being. Now either absolutely

[1] Omitting *μήν*.

[2] Reading *τῷ κατὰ φύσιν ἐναντίον· ἡ οὖν κατὰ φύσιν γένεσις*, with Vitelli.

all animals belong to the class of things that have come into being by nature,[1] or the best and most honourable of them do; for it makes no difference if someone thinks most animals have come into being contrary to nature, to destroy and do mischief. Now man is the most honourable of the animals in the world, so that clearly he has come into being by nature and according to nature; and knowledge is that for the sake of which nature and God have brought us into being. Pythagoras, when asked what this end is, said 'to observe the heavens', and used to say he was an observer of nature and it was for this that he had come into being. And they say that Anaxagoras, when asked for what end one would choose to come into being and to live, replied 'to observe the heavens and the stars, moon, and sun in them', everything else being nothing worth. If, then, the end of each thing is always better than the thing (for everything that comes into being does so for the sake of its end, and its end is better and the best of all things), and if that which is completed last in order of generation when this proceeds continuously is the natural end, we note that the bodily parts of men are completed first and the mental parts later, and the completion of the better is, one may say, always later than its generation. Therefore soul is later than body, and wisdom is the latest of the qualities of the soul; for we see that by nature it is the latest faculty to come into being for men—that is why old age lays special claim to this alone of good things; therefore some form of wisdom is by nature our end, and the exercise of it the final activity for whose sake we have come into being. Now if we have come into being in order to exercise it and to learn, we also exist for that end. According to this argument, then, Pythagoras was right in saying that every man has been created by God in order to know and to observe. But whether the object of this knowlege is the world or something whose nature is different, we must consider later; what we have said suffices as a first conclusion; for if wisdom is our natural end, the exercise of it must be the best of all things. Therefore the other things we ought to do, we ought to do for the sake of the goods that come

[1] Reading in τῶν φύσει γεγενημένων, with the MSS.

into being in oneself,[1] and of these the bodily actions should be done for the sake of the mental, and virtue should be practised for the sake of wisdom; for this is the supreme end.

12 (R[3] 58, W 12)

AUG. *Trin.* 14. 9. 12. Cicero in his dialogue *Hortensius* argues thus: 'If we, when we depart[2] this life, were permitted to live for ever, as the fables say, in the islands of the blest, what need should we have of eloquence when there were no causes to be pleaded—or even of the virtues themselves? We should not need courage, where no task or danger was prescribed to us, nor justice, where there was no property of another for us to seek, nor temperance, to rule non-existent lusts. We should not need even prudence, where no choice between goods and evils was held out to us. We should be blessed by the possession of one thing only—science and knowledge of nature, for which alone the life of the gods is to be praised. From this it may be seen that other things are matters of necessity, and only this a matter of choice. Thus that great orator, when he was preaching philosophy by repeating and expounding splendidly and persuasively what he had received from the philosophers, said that it is only in this life, which we see to be full of cares and errors, that all the four virtues are necessary.

IAMBL. *Protr.* 9 (52. 16–54. 5 Pistelli). To seek from all knowledge a result other than itself, and to demand that knowledge must be useful, is the act of one completely ignorant of the distance that from the start separates things good from things necessary; they stand at opposite extremes. For of the things without which life is impossible those that are loved for the sake of something else must be called necessities and contributing causes, but those that are loved for themselves even if nothing follows must be called goods in the strict sense. This is not desirable for the sake of that, and that for the sake of something else, and so *ad infinitum*; there is a stop somewhere. It is completely ridiculous, therefore, to

[1] Reading αὑτῷ.
[2] Reading in R. 68. 3 *emigraverimus*, with the MSS.

demand from everything some benefit other than the thing itself, and to ask 'What then is the gain to us?' and 'What is the use?' For in truth, as we maintain, he who asks this is in no way like one who knows the noble and good, or who distinguishes causes from accompanying conditions. One would see the supreme truth of what we are saying, if someone[1] carried us in thought to the islands of the blest. There there would be need of nothing, no profit from anything; there remain only thought and contemplation, which even now we describe as the free life. If this be true, would not any of us be rightly ashamed if when the chance was given us to live in the islands of the blest, he were by his own fault unable to do so? Not to be despised, therefore, is the reward that knowledge brings to men, nor slight the good that comes from it. For as, according to the wise among the poets, we receive the gifts of justice in Hades, so (it seems) we gain those of wisdom in the islands of the blest. It is nowise strange, then, if wisdom does not show itself useful or advantageous; we call it not advantageous but good, it should be chosen not for the sake of anything else, but for itself. For as we travel to Olympia for the sake of the spectacle itself, even if nothing were to follow from it (for the spectacle itself is worth more than much wealth), and as we view the Dionysia not in order to gain anything from the actors (indeed we spend money on them), and as there are many other spectacles we should prefer to much wealth, so too the contemplation of the universe is to be honoured above all the things that are thought useful. For surely it cannot be right that we should take great pains to go to see men imitating women and slaves, or fighting and running, just for the sake of the spectacle, and not think it right to view without payment the nature and reality of things.

13 (W 13)

IAMBL. *Protr.* 10 (54. 10–56. 12 Pistelli). That theoretical wisdom also provides us with the greatest advantages for

[1] Reading after *λέγομεν* in R. 69. 1 *οὐδεν ἔοικεν ὁ τοιοῦτος εἰδότι καλὸν κἀγαθὸν οὐδὲ τί αἴτιον τῷ διαγιγνώσκοντι καὶ συναίτιον. ἴδοι δ' ἄν τις ὅτι παντὸς μᾶλλον ἀληθῆ ταῦτα λέγομεν, εἴ τις κτλ.*, with the MSS.

human life, one will discover easily from studying the arts. For as all skilful physicians and most gymnasts agree that those who are to be good physicians or gymnasts must have experience of nature, so it is agreed that good legislators must have experience of nature, and indeed much more than the former. For the former are producers only of bodily excellence, while those who are concerned with the excellences of the soul and undertake to give instruction about the well-being and the ill-being of the state need philosophy far more. As in the mechanical arts the best instruments have been borrowed from nature (e.g. in carpentry the ruddled line, the rule, and the lathe were suggested by the surface of water and by the rays of light,[1] and it is by reference to these that we test what is to our senses sufficiently straight or smooth), similarly the statesman must borrow from nature and reality certain limits by reference to which he will judge what is just, noble, or advantageous; for as these tools excel all others, so the law that conforms best with nature is the best. Now this he cannot do unless he has practised philosophy and learned the truth. And in the other arts men do not take their tools and their most accurate calculations from the originals themselves and so attain something approaching to knowledge; they take them from copies at second or third hand or at a distant remove, and base their reasonings on experience. The philosopher alone copies the exact originals; he is a spectator of them and not of copies. As, then, he is not a good builder who does not use a straight rule or any other such instrument but compares his own building with others, so, presumably, if one either lays down laws for cities or does actions of his own, looking to and copying other actions or human constitutions, whether of Sparta or of Crete or of any other state, he is not a good lawgiver nor a virtuous man; for an imitation of what is not good cannot be good, nor can an imitation of what is not divine and durable in its nature be immortal and durable; it is clear[2] that to the philosopher alone among craftsmen belong laws that are durable and actions that are right and

[1] The text is corrupt, but the general sense is clear.
[2] Reading ἀλλὰ δῆλον ὅτι κτλ., with Vitelli.

noble. For he alone lives with his eye on nature and the divine, and like a good steersman directs his life[1] in dependence on what is eternal and unchanging, and lives his own master. This knowledge is theoretical indeed, but it enables us to frame all our practice in accordance with it. For as sight makes and shapes nothing (since its only work is to judge and to show us everything that can be seen), and yet it enables us to act as it directs, and gives us the greatest assistance towards action (for we should be almost entirely motionless if deprived of it), so it is clear that, though knowledge is theoretical, yet we do a host of things in accordance with it, choose some actions and avoid others, and in general gain as a result of it all the goods we possess.

14 (W 14)

IAMB. *Protr.* 11 (56. 13–59. 18 Pistelli). That those who have chosen the life according to reason also enjoy life most will be clear from the following argument. The word 'live' seems to be used in two senses, one implying a potentiality, the other an actuality; for we describe as 'seeing' both those animals which have sight and are born capable of seeing, even if they happen to have their eyes shut, and those which are using this faculty and looking definitely at something. Similarly with cognition or knowing; we sometimes mean by it the use of the faculty, actual contemplation, and sometimes the possession of the faculty of knowledge. If, then, we distinguish life from non-life by the possession of perception, and 'perception' has two meanings, meaning properly the using of the senses, but in another significance the being able to use them (it is for this reason, it seems, that we say even a sleeping man perceives),[2] it is clear that 'live' will correspondingly have two meanings; a waking man must be said to live in the true and proper sense, a sleeping man must be said to live because he is capable of passing into the activity in virtue of which we say that a man is waking and perceiving something; it is for this reason and with reference

[1] Reading ὁρμᾷ, with the MSS.

[2] It is not necessary to assume the existence of a lacuna here. For φαμὲν λέγοντες cf. L. and S. s.v. φημί II. 2.

to this that we describe him as living.[1] When, therefore, each of two things is called by the same name, and one of the two is so called by virtue of acting or being acted on,[2] we shall assign the name by preference to this one; we shall use the word 'know' rather of him who is using than of him who merely possesses knowledge, and 'see' rather of him who is directing his sight than of him who merely can do so. For we apply the comparative degree not only to that which possesses more completely an attribute that has a single definition, but also to that whose possession of the attribute is prior; e.g. we say that health is better than wholesome things, and that which is by its own nature worthy of choice than that which tends to produce this, though we see that it is not by virtue of the definition's being predicable of both that we describe both useful things and virtue as good. Thus we must assign life in a higher degree to a waking man than to a sleeping one, to a man who is exercising his soul than to one who merely possesses a soul; for it is because of the former that we assign life also to the latter, because he is such as to act, or be acted on, in the former way.[3] The exercising of anything, then, is this: if the faculty admits only of one realization, it is exercised when one does just that thing; if the faculty admits of more than one realization, it is exercised when one brings about its best realization; e.g. one uses the flute either only, or most completely, when one is actually playing it; for presumably it is on the basis of this that the 'uses' of it by other people are called uses. So we must say that he who uses a thing aright uses it in a higher degree, since the natural purpose[4] and the natural manner belong to the man who uses the thing well and accurately. Now thinking and reasoning are, either alone or above everything else, the work of the soul. It is a simple inference, one that anyone can easily draw, that the man who thinks aright lives in a higher degree than others, that he who reaches truth in the highest degree lives in the

[1] Placing the full stop after *βλέποντες*, not after *τινος*.
[2] Reading *τῷ ποιεῖν ἢ τῷ πάσχειν*, with the MSS.
[3] Reading *ἐκείνως*, as suggested by Pistelli.
[4] Reading *ἐφ' ὅ*, with the MSS.

highest degree, and that this is the man who thinks and theorizes according to the most precise knowledge; and it is then and to these men that living completely must be ascribed—to those who think and to those who have the capacity to think. Now if living is, alike for every animal, its true being, it is clear that the thinker will *be* in the highest degree and in the most proper sense, and most of all when he is exercising this faculty and contemplating what is the most knowable of all things. But further, perfect and unimpeded activity contains in itself delight, so that the activity of contemplation must be the most pleasant of all. Further, there is a difference between enjoying oneself while drinking and enjoying drinking; for there is nothing to prevent a man who is not thirsty, or is not getting the drink he enjoys, from enjoying himself while drinking, not because he is drinking but because he happens at the same time to be looking at something, or to be looked at, as he sits. So we shall say that such a man enjoys himself, and enjoys himself while drinking, but not because he is drinking, nor that he is enjoying drinking. In the same way we shall say that walking, sitting down, learning, any activity, is pleasant or painful, not if we happen to feel pain or pleasure in the presence of these activities, but if we are all pained or pleased by their presence. Similarly we shall call that life pleasant whose presence is pleasant to those who have it; we shall say that not all who have pleasure while living enjoy living, but only those to whom life itself is pleasant and who rejoice in the pleasure that comes from living. Now we assign life to the man who is awake rather than to him who is asleep, to him who thinks rather than to him who is thoughtless, and we say the pleasure of living is the pleasure we get from the exercise of the soul; that is true life. If, then, there are more than one exercise of the soul, still the chief of all is that of thinking as well as possible.[1] It is clear, then, that the pleasure arising from thinking and contemplation is, alone or most of all, the pleasure of living. Pleasant life and enjoyment, therefore, belong in truth only to philosophers, or to them most of all. For the activity of our truest

[1] Reading ὅτι μάλιστα, with Walzer.

thoughts, that which is replenished from the most real realities, and preserves steadfastly for ever the perfection it receives, this is of all activities the most productive of joy. Thus even for the sake of enjoying true and good pleasures men of sense ought to practise philosophy.

15 (W 15)

IAMBL. *Protr.* 12 (59. 19–60. 15 Pistelli). If we ought to draw this conclusion not only from considering the elements of well-being, but also start higher up and establish it by considering well-being as a whole, let us say explicitly that as philosophizing is related to well-being, so is it related to the acquisition by us of anything good or bad. For it is as leading to this or as following from it that the existence of anything is for all men worthy of desire, and some of the things through which we have well-being are such because they are necessary, some because they are pleasant. Now we define well-being either as thoughtfulness (a sort of wisdom), or as virtue, or as the extreme of enjoyment, or as all of these together. If it is thoughtfulness, clearly philosophers alone will live happily; if it is excellence of the soul or enjoyment, then, too, it will belong to them alone or most of all; for the highest element in us is virtue, and thinking is the most pleasant of all single things. Similarly, if one says that all these things together are well-being, well-being must be defined as thinking.[1]

Therefore all who can should practise philosophy; for this is either complete good life, or of all single things most truly the cause of good life for souls. In this world, I suppose because life in it is unnatural to our race, learning and insight are difficult, and perception scarcely to be obtained[2] because of our awkward and unnatural mode of life; but if we can ever escape back to the place from which we have come, it is clear that we shall all do these things more pleasantly and more easily.

16 (R[2] 77, R[3] 90, W 16)

ATH. 335 f. . . . enjoying the life of Sardanapallus, son of

[1] Reading τῷ φρονεῖν.

[2] Reading μόλις ἂν αἰσθάνοιτο, suggested by Pistelli.

Anacyndaraxes, whom Aristotle described as even sillier than[1] the name of his father would suggest.

CIC. *Tusc.* 5. 35. 101. How then can a life be pleasant from which prudence and moderation are absent? We see from this the error of Sardanapallus, the wealthy king of Syria, who ordered these words to be engraved on his tomb: 'What I ate and what sated lust drained to the dregs, that I have; many a famous deed lies left behind.' 'What else', Aristotle says, 'would you have inscribed on the grave, not of a king but of an ox? He says he had in death the things which even in life he had no longer than for the moment of enjoyment.'

Cf. STRABO 14. 5. 9, p. C 672; CIC. *Fin.* 2. 32. 106.

17 (R[3] 54)

CHALC. *in Tim.* 208–9 (Wrobel). In this Aristotle also agrees, saying that children at first, while still unweaned, think all men their fathers and all women their mothers, but as they grow up come to draw distinctions, and yet sometimes fail to do so, since they are often taken in by false images and hold out their hands to a mere simulacrum. He calls all these opinions unmanly; those who hold them think that the things that hurt us are beneficial and those that help us noxious; they are led towards pleasure that destroys, and take offence at healthy toil. This would certainly never have happened if they had not trusted too much to the senses, which by nature are most lively when they deceive. To make the whole matter plain, Aristotle uses an example of crystal clearness. The height of madness is reached when a man not only is ignorant, but does not know what he is ignorant of, and therefore gives his assent to false images and takes those that are true to be false; as when men think that vice profits them and virtue acts to their prejudice and ruin. . . . These men Aristotle calls old children, because their mind differs very little from a child's.

[1] Reading in R. 91. 2 εἶναι ἢ κατά, with Madvig.

18 (W 18)

Cic. *Tusc.* 5. 30. 85. The case of the Peripatetics has been unfolded—apart from the views of Theophrastus and those who, following him, show a weak dread of and shrinking from pain; the rest may do what they in fact practically do, to exaggerate the importance and dignity of virtue. When they have extolled it to the skies, which these eloquent men are wont to do at length . . . 31. 87 according to the reasoning of these men the happy life will follow virtue even if it leads to torture, and will descend with it into the tyrant's bull,[1] with Aristotle, Xenocrates, Speusippus, and Polemon, to encourage it; it will never, seduced by threats or blandishments, desert virtue.

Ibid. 5. 10. 30. I do not, therefore, readily allow my friend Brutus, or our common masters, or the ancients, Aristotle, Speusippus, Xenocrates, and Polemon, when they count as evils the things I have enumerated above, at the same time to say that the 'wise man' is always happy. If this noble and beautiful title, most worthy of Pythagoras, Socrates, and Plato, delights them, let them bring themselves to despise the things by whose splendour they are attracted—strength, health, beauty, riches, honours, power—and to count their opposites as nothing; then they will be able with a voice of crystal clearness to profess that they are terrified neither by the onslaught of fortune, by the opinion of the multitude, by pain, nor by poverty, that everything lies in themselves, that there is nothing outside their power which they should reckon as a good.

Cf. ibid. 5. 13. 39.

Cic. *Fin.* 5. 5. 12. But since the happy life is sought for, and the one thing that philosophy ought to consider and pursue is the question whether happiness is entirely in the power of the wise man, or whether it can be weakened or snatched from

[1] Phalaris' brazen bull.

him by adversity, on this point there seems to be sometimes variation and doubt among philosophers. This impression is produced most strongly by Theophrastus' book on the happy life, in which a great deal is ascribed to fortune. If this were true, wisdom could not guarantee a happy life. This seems to me, so to speak, a softer and more timid line of thought than that demanded by the force and dignity of virtue. Let us, therefore, cling to Aristotle and his son Nicomachus . . . but let us follow Theophrastus in most things, only allowing virtue more firmness and strength than he did. . . . 14 Our own Antiochus seems to me to follow most faithfully the opinion of the ancients, which was (he maintains) common to Aristotle[1] and to Polemon.

19 (R³ 25, W 19)

CENSOR. c. 18. 11. There is, too, a year which Aristotle calls not the great but the greatest, which the spheres of the sun, the moon, and the five planets complete when they return together to the same constellation with which they were formerly in conjunction.

CIC. *N.D.* 2. 20. 51–52. Most admirable are the motions of the five stars which we wrongly call wandering stars. . . . It is on the basis of their diverse motions that mathematicians have given the name of 'great year' to that which is completed when the sun, the moon, and the five 'wandering' stars, the course of all of them completed, have returned to the same relative positions. How long this period is, is a great question, but it must be certain and definite.

Cf. CIC. *Hortensius*, fr. 35 Müller; TAC. *Dial.* 16. 7.

20

TERT. *De An.* 46. How many writers have commented on this matter[2] and asserted its existence—Artemon, Antiphon,

[1] Reading *Aristotelis*, with some MSS.
[2] sc. interpretation of dreams.

Strato, Philochorus, Epicharmus, Serapion, Cratippus, Dionysius Rhodius, Hermippus, the whole literature of the age! If I laugh at anyone it will be at the writer who thought he could persuade us that Saturn was the first to dream; he could be this only if he was the first to live. Aristotle, pardon my laughter!

ON WEALTH

1 (R^2 86, R^3 56)

PLU. *Pel.* 3. 1. Of the general run of people, as Aristotle says, some through meanness do not use their wealth, others through extravagance misuse it; the latter are permanent slaves to their pleasures, the former to their business.

PLU. *Mor.* 527 a. Aristotle says that some men do not use wealth, others misuse it, implying that both are wrong; the former get no benefit or grace from what they have, the latter derive injury and disgrace.

2 (R^2 87, R^3 89)

CIC. *Off.* 2. 16. 56–57. How much more weight and truth there is in Aristotle's reproach to us for not wondering at these lavish sums spent on cajoling the mob! That men besieged by an enemy should be forced into paying a mina for a pint of water, that (he says) seems incredible when we first hear of it, and we all marvel at it, but when we consider it we pardon their necessity; in these vast and boundless expenditures there is nothing that much surprises us, and that though there is no relief of necessity, no increase of dignity, and the very delight of the multitude is shortlived and derived from the meanest objects, and when satiation comes the very memory of the pleasure dies. He sums up the matter well when he says these things gratify children and mere women, slaves and freemen who are like slaves, but can in no way be approved by a serious man who weighs events with solid judgement.

3

PHILOD. *Pap. Herc.* 3, p. 41, col. 211. Which happened to Aristotle (as Metrodorus proved) in respect of the argument, in the work *On Wealth*, to show that the good man is also a good money-maker, and the bad man a bad money-maker.

ON PRAYER

I (R^2 46, R^3 49, W I)

SIMP. *in De Caelo* 485. 19–22. That Aristotle has the notion of something above reason and being is shown by his saying clearly, at the end of his book *On Prayer*, that God is either reason or something even beyond reason.

ON GOOD BIRTH

1 (R^2 82, R^3 91)

STOB. 4. 29 A 24. From Aristotle *On Good Birth*. 'With regard to good birth, I for my part am quite at a loss to say whom one should call well-born.'

'Your difficulty', I said, 'is quite natural; for both among the many and even more among the wise there is division of opinion and obscurity of statement, particularly about the significance of good birth. What I mean is this: Is it a precious and good thing, or, as Lycophron the sophist wrote,[1] something altogether trivial? Comparing it with other goods, he says the attractiveness of good birth is obscure, and its dignity a matter of words; i.e. that the preference for it is a matter of opinion, and in truth there is no difference between the low-born and the well-born.'

2 (R^2 83, R^3 92)

STOB. 4. 29 A 25. In the same book. 'Just as it is disputed what size is good,[2] so it is disputed who those are who ought to be called well-born. Some think it is those born of good ancestors, which was the view of Socrates; he said that because Aristides was good his daughter was nobly born. They say that Simonides, when asked who it is that are well-born, said "those whose family has long been rich"; but at that rate Theognis' caustic observation is wrong, and so is that of the poet who wrote "Mortals honour good birth, but marry rather with the rich".[3] Good heavens, is not a man who is rich himself preferable to one who had a rich great-grandfather or some other rich ancestor, but is himself poor?'

'Surely,' he said.

'And one ought to marry with the rich rather than with the well-born; for it is people of long ago that were well-

[1] Reading in R. 92. 4 Λυκόφρων ὁ σοφιστὴς ἔγραφε, with the MSS.

[2] sc. in any given type of thing.

[3] Eur. fr. 399 Nauck.

born, but people of today that are more powerful. Is it not much the same, then, if one supposes that it is not those born of rich ancestors but those born of good ancestors that are well-born? One would suppose that recent goodness is better than ancient, that a man has more in common with his father than with his great-grandfather, and that it is preferable to be good oneself rather than to have a great-grandfather or some other ancestor who was good.'

'You are right,' he said.

'Well then, since we see that good birth does not consist in either of these things, should we not look elsewhere to see what it consists in?'

'We should,' he said.

'"Good" means, I suppose, something praiseworthy and excellent; e.g. having a good face or good eyes means, on this showing, something excellent or beautiful.'

'Certainly,' he said.

'Well then, having a good face means having the goodness proper to a face, and having good eyes means having the goodness proper to eyes, does it not?'

'Yes,' he said.

'But one stock is good, another bad and not good.'

'Certainly,' he said.

'And we say each thing is good in virtue of the excellence proper to it, so that a stock is good in the same way.'

'Yes,' he said.

'Clearly, then,' I said, 'good birth is excellence of stock.'

3 (R^2 84, R^3 93)

DIOG. LAERT. 2. 5. 26 (10). Aristotle says Socrates married two wives—first Xanthippe, who bore him Lamprocles, and then Myrto, daughter of Aristides the Just, whom he took though she had no dowry, and who bore him Sophroniscus and Menexenus.

PLU. *Aristid.* 27. 2. Demetrius of Phaleron, Hieronymus of Rhodes, Aristoxenus the writer on music, and Aristotle (if the work *On Good Birth* is to be reckoned among his genuine works) relate that Myrto, granddaughter of Aristides, lived with the Sage Socrates, who was married to another woman but took Myrto under his protection because she was a widow, poor and lacking in the necessities of life.

Ath. 555 d–556 a. Starting from these facts, one must blame those who assign to Socrates two wedded wives, Xanthippe and Myrto the daughter of Aristides—not Aristides the Just, for the dates do not permit of this, but the third in descent from him. These writers are Callisthenes, Demetrius of Phaleron, Satyrus the Peripatetic, Aristoxenus; Aristotle gave them the keynote by relating this in his work *On Good Birth.*

4 (R^2 85, R^3 94)

Stob. 4. 29 c 52. From Aristotle's work *On Good Birth.* 'It is evident, then', I said, 'from our previous discussion, why those born of a long line of rich or good ancestors are thought to be better born than those whose possession of these advantages is recent. A man's own goodness is nearer to him than that of a grandfather, and on that basis it would be the good man that is well-born. And some writers have said this, claiming to disprove by this argument the merits of good birth; Euripides, for example, says[1] that good birth belongs not to those whose ancestors have long been good, but to him who is himself good, simply. That is not so; those are right who give the preference to ancient virtue. Let us state the reasons for this. Good birth is excellence of stock, and excellence belongs to good men; and a good stock is one in which there have been many good men. Now this happens when the stock has had a good origin; for an origin has the power of producing many products like itself; this is the function of an origin—to produce many results like itself. When, then, there has been one man of this kind in the stock, a man so good that many generations inherit his goodness, that stock is bound to be good. There will be many good men if the stock is human, many good horses if it is equine,

[1] fr. 345 Nauck.

and so too with the other animals. Thus it is natural that not rich men nor good men, but those whose ancestors have long been rich or good, should be well-born. The argument has its eye on the truth; the origin counts more than anything else. Yet not even those born of good ancestors are in every case well-born, but only those who have among their ancestors originators. When a man is good himself, but has not the natural power to beget many like him, the origin has not in such a case the power we have ascribed to it.

'... People are well-born if they come of such a stock—not if their father is well-born, but if the originator of the stock is so. For it is not by his own strength that a father begets a good man, but because he came of such a stock.'

ON PLEASURE

1[1] (R^2 72, R^3 83)

ATH. 6 d. Others call Philoxenus a fish-lover, but Aristotle calls him simply a dinner-lover. He also writes somewhere as follows: 'When they are making speeches to crowded audiences they spend the whole day in relating marvels, and that to people who have just returned from the Phasis or the Borysthenes,[2] when they have themselves read nothing but Philoxenus' *Banquet*, and not the whole of that.'

[1] Rose places this fragment under the work *On Justice*, but it seems to have no connexion with that subject. It is in connexion with the love of bodily pleasures that Philoxenus is mentioned in *Eth. Eud.* 1231^{a}5–17, and alluded to in *Eth. Nic.* 1118^{a}32–^{b}1, so that the description of him as a dinner-lover is more likely to have occurred in the dialogue *On Pleasure*. In what work of Aristotle the words actually quoted by Athenaeus occurred, it is impossible to say.

[2] The Rion or the Dnieper.

ON EDUCATION

1 (R^2 51, R^3 62)

PLU. *Mor.* 734 d. Florus was full of problems himself, and he used to share them with his associates, bearing witness to Aristotle's saying that much learning brings many vexations.

2 (R^2 52, R^3 63)

DIOG. LAERT. 9. 8. 53 (4). Protagoras was the first to discover the so-called 'knot' on which porters carry their burdens—so Aristotle says in his work *On Education*; for Protagoras was a porter, as Epicurus also says somewhere. It was in this way that Protagoras was brought to the notice of Democritus, who saw how he had bound his logs together.

Cf. ATH. 354 c.

ON KINGSHIP

TESTIMONIA

CIC. *Att.* 12. 40. 2. I often try a letter of advice;[1] I find nothing to say. I have, indeed, with me the books both of Aristotle and of Theopompus addressed to Alexander. But what resemblance is there? They wrote what was both honourable to them and acceptable to Alexander; do you find anything of that sort here?

Ibid. 13. 28. 2. Nothing comes into my mind. You see what the advice sent to Alexander by eloquent and learned men is concerned with. They exhort to honourable conduct[2] a young man kindled by desire for the truest glory, wishing for some advice that shall redound to his eternal praise.

PS.-AMM. *in Cat.* (Ven. 1546, f. 9 *b*). Those works are 'personal' which were written to some individual in particular, as for instance letters or what Aristotle wrote at the request of Alexander of Macedon about kingship and about the right way of establishing colonies.

1 (R^2 78, R^3 646)

PS.-AMM. *in Cat.* (Ven. 1546, f. 5 *b*). Aristotle wrote to Alexander also about kingship, in a one-volume book, instructing him how he ought to rule.

Vit. Arist Marc. p. 430. 15–431. 2 (Rose). In order to confer a benefit on all men, Aristotle writes a book addressed to Alexander on kingship, instructing him how he should rule. This had such an effect on Alexander's mind that when he had failed to confer a benefit on anyone he said: 'Today I have not been king; I have done good to no one.'

[1] To Caesar.

[2] Reading in R. 408. 24 *cohortantur ad decus*, with the MSS.

2 (R[2] 79, R[3] 647)

THEM. *Or.* 107 c–d. Plato, even if in all other respects he was divine and admirable, was completely reckless when he uttered this saying, that evils would never cease for men until either philosophers became rulers, or kings became philosophers. His saying has been refuted and has paid its account to time. We should do honour to Aristotle, who slightly altered Plato's words and made his counsel truer; he said that it was not merely unnecessary for a king to be a philosopher, but even a disadvantage; what he should do was to listen to and take the advice of true philosophers, since then he filled his reign with good deeds, not with good words.

ALEXANDER

1 (R^2 80, R^3 648)

Ps.-Amm. *in Cat.* (Ven. 1546, f. 9 *b*). See p. 65 *supra*.

2 (R^2 81, R^3 658)

Plu. *Mor.* 329 *b*. Alexander did not do as Aristotle advised—play the part of a leader to the Greeks and of a master to the barbarians, care for the former as friends and kinsmen, and treat the latter as beasts or plants, and so fill his reign with wars, banishments, and factions; he behaved alike to all.

Strabo i. 4. 9, p. C 66. At the conclusion of his memorandum, Eratosthenes refuses to praise those who divided the whole human race into two—Greeks and barbarians—and advised Alexander to treat Greeks as friends, but barbarians as enemies; he says it is better to draw the division between virtue and vice. . . . Alexander did not ignore his advisers but took their advice and acted accordingly, looking to the intention of those who had sent it.

POLITICUS

TESTIMONIUM

CIC. *Fin.* 5. 4. 11. Aristotle and Theophrastus had, each of them, taught what sort of man the ruler in a state should be.

1 (R^2 70, R^3 78)

CIC. *Q. Fr.* 3. 5. 1. When these books were being read over to me in my Tusculan villa in the hearing of Sallust, I was advised by him that something much more authoritative could be said on these matters if I were myself to speak about the state; especially because I was not a Heraclides Ponticus but a man of consular rank and one versed in the greatest affairs of state. What I put into the mouth of such ancient authorities would be seen to be fictitious. . . . Finally, he remarked that Aristotle himself says in his own name what he has to say about the state and the rule of it by the outstanding[1] man.

2 (R^3 79)

SYRIAN. *in Metaph.* 168. 33–35. At all events Aristotle in the second book of his *Politicus* says expressly . . . 'The good is the most accurate measure of all things'.

3 (R^2 94–95, R^3 80)

SEN. *De Ira* 1. 3. 3. Aristotle's definition is not far removed from ours; he says anger is the desire to repay pain.

Ibid. 1. 9. 2. Anger, Aristotle says, is necessary, nor can any battle be won without it—unless it fills the mind and kindles the spirit. But we must treat it not as a commander but as a soldier.

[1] Reading *praestanti*, with Wesenberg.

Ibid. 1. 17. 1. Aristotle says certain passions serve as weapons, if we use them aright.

Ibid. 3. 3. 1. But, as I have said in former books, Aristotle stands as the defender of anger and forbids the expulsion of it from our nature. He says it is the spur to virtue, and if it is taken from us the mind becomes unarmed, and too sluggish and inert for great endeavours. . . 5. There is, then, no reason why you should think that I am wasting time on useless matters, and that anger is disgraceful, as though it were a thing of doubtful repute among men, when there is someone, a famous philosopher indeed, who assigns definite functions to it, and invokes it as useful, and as supplying spirit for battle, for active life, for everything that demands a certain heat.

Ibid. 1. 7. 1. Is anger to be called to our aid? It has often been useful. It raises and excites the spirits; courage does nothing splendid in war without it—nothing unless it is inflamed by anger, unless anger has goaded men into boldness in face of danger. Some therefore think it best to temper anger, not to root it out; to reduce it to healthy proportions by eradicating what is excessive, but to retain that without which action would languish and the force and vigour of the mind be relaxed.

Cic. *Tusc.* 4. 19. 43. What shall we say of the Peripatetic view that those perturbations which *we* think should be extirpated are not only natural, but even a useful gift of nature? This is what they say: First, they say much in praise of anger; they call it the whetstone of courage and say that, whether it be against an enemy or against a bad citizen, the reaction of an angry man is far more vigorous. They make light of the petty reasonings of those whose thoughts took this form: 'It is right that this battle be fought; it is fitting to fight for law, for liberty, for country.' These thoughts, they say, have no force unless courage is fanned into a blaze by anger. Nor do they argue only about soldiers in battle; they think no strict discipline is possible without some bitterness of anger. Finally, they think little of a speaker unless, in defence as well as in attack, he feels the sting of anger. Even if anger is not there, they think it must be simulated in language and in gesture, that the speaker's action may kindle the hearer's anger. In short, they say he seems no man who does not know how to be angry, and what we call mildness they call by the opprobrious name of sluggishness. Nor, indeed, is it only *this* craving that they praise—for anger, as I have just defined it, is craving for revenge—they say that craving or desire in general is a most useful gift of nature, since no one can do supremely well what he does not desire to do. . . . 20. 45. They say that pain itself . . . is established by nature to a most useful end, in order that in their ill-doing men should feel the suffering of punishment, blame, and disgrace. For those who bear without pain disgrace and infamy seem to be granted immunity for their sins; it is better to suffer the gnawing of conscience. . . . 46. They say the other forms of pain also have their uses; pity leads men to help others and relieve undeserved suffering; even envy and disparagement are not without use, when one sees that one has gained less than another, or that another has gained as much as oneself; if anyone took from us fear, he would take with it all diligence, which is greatest in those who fear the laws, the magistrates, poverty, disgrace, death, pain. In their discussions they admit that desires must be pruned, but say that they neither can nor need be completely uprooted, and that in almost all things the mean is the best.

PHILOD. *De Ira*, p. 65. 31–66. 2 (Wilke). Some at least of the Peripatetics, as we have previously indicated by reference to individuals, say that those who remove anger and temper cut outright the sinews of the soul; that without these things there would be neither punishment nor vengeance . . . that men would not engage in wars without anger, which makes them bold and takes away all shrinking and cowardice, and makes men steadfast even to death. So, too, anger produces the spirit of vengeance on enemies,[1] the existence of which

[1] Reading in R. 84. 33–85. 1 τιμωρητικὸν τῶν ἐχθρῶν, with Wilke.

is noble, just, privately and publicly advantageous, and pleasant to boot.

4

PHILOD. *Voll. Rhet.* 2. 175, fr. 15. 1–6. A hare that makes its appearance among hounds cannot escape (Aristotle says), nor can that which is deemed shameless and despicable survive among men.

5

PAP. HERC. 1020. From these facts, they say, it follows that wise men (as Aristotle says) cannot be deceived or err, and do all things well.

ON POETS

TESTIMONIA

ARIST. *Poet.* $1454^{b}15$–18. All these rules one must keep in mind throughout, and, further, those also for such points of stage-effect as directly depend on the art of the poet, since in these too one may often make mistakes. Enough, however, has been said on the subject in our published writings.

Vita Arist. Marciana p. 427. 3–7 (Rose). While he was still young, he received the education of a free man, as is shown by his *Homeric Questions*, by the edition of the *Iliad* which he gave to Alexander, by the dialogue *On Poets*, the *Poetics*, and the rhetorical treatises.

Cf. *Vita Arist.* vulgo (ante ps.-Ammon. *in Cat.*).

DIO CHR. *Or.* 53. 1: see p. 3 *supra*.

1 (R^2 59, R^3 70)

DIOG. LAERT. 8. 2. 57–58 (3). In his work *On Poets* Aristotle describes Empedocles as Homeric, and an artist in language, skilled in metaphor and in the other devices of poetry; he adds that Empedocles wrote, besides other poems, one on Xerxes' crossing of the Hellespont, and a prelude to Apollo, but that a sister—or, as Hieronymus says, a daughter—burned the prelude by accident, and the Persian poem intentionally, because it was unfinished. Aristotle adds, in general terms, that he also wrote tragedies and works on politics.

2 (R^2 60, R^3 71)

DIOG. LAERT. 8. 2. 51–52 (1). Empedocles, according to Hippobotus, was the son of Meton son of Empedocles, and belonged to Agrigentum. . . . Eratosthenes in his list of

Olympic winners says that Meton's father was successful in the seventy-first Olympiad; his authority is Aristotle. Apollodorus the grammarian in his chronicles says Empedocles 'was the son of Meton, and Glaucus says he went to Thurii just after its foundation'. Then a little later he says: 'Those who relate that he fled from home to Syracuse and fought with the Syracusans against the Athenians seem to me to be completely mistaken; for he was either no longer alive or in extreme old age, which, however, does not seem to have been the case. For Aristotle and also Heraclides say he died at the age of sixty.' The Empedocles who won a horse-race in the seventy-first Olympiad was his grandfather and namesake, so that Apollodorus indicates his date as well as his parentage.

Cf. ibid. 8. 2. 74 (11).

3 (R[2] 61, R[3] 72)

DIOG. LAERT. 3. 48 (32). It is said that Zeno the Eleatic was the first to write dialogues; but Aristotle in the first book of his work *On Poets* says it was Alexamenos of Styra or of Teos, as Favorinus also says in his *Memoirs*. But Plato seems to me, by bringing the genre to perfection, to deserve the first prize for the invention, as well as for the beauty of his execution.

ATH. 505 b–c. The writer who has utterly condemned the others[1] recounts the praises of Meno; in the *Republic* he banishes Homer and imitative poetry, but he himself wrote his dialogues in an imitative way. He was not even the inventor of this type; for before him Alexamenos of Teos invented this type of writing, as Nicias of Nicaea and Sotion testify. Aristotle in his work *On Poets* writes thus: 'Are we then to deny that the so-called mimes of Sophron, which are not even in metre,[2] are stories and imitations, or the dialogues of Alexamenos of Teos, which were written before[3]

[1] i.e. Plato.
[2] Reading in R. 78. 11 *ἐμμέτρους ὄντας τούς*, with Kaibel.
[3] Reading in R. 78. 13 *πρότερον*, suggested by Kaibel.

the Socratic dialogues?' Thus the great savant Aristotle says outright that Alexamenos wrote dialogues before Plato.

4 (R² 62, R³ 73)

DIOG. LAERT. 3. 37 (25). Aristotle says that the genre of Plato's dialogues lies between poetry and prose.

5 (R² 63, R³ 81)

PROCL. *in Remp.* I. 42. 2 (Kroll). We must first mention and discuss Plato's reason for not admitting poetry. . . . 10. Secondly, what can be the reason why he specially excludes tragedy and comedy, though these contribute to the purification of the passions, which can neither be completely repelled nor safely gratified to the full, but need seasonable exercise, the achievement of which in listening to drama saves us from being troubled by them at other times? . . . 49. 13. The second point was that the expulsion of tragedy and comedy is paradoxical, since by means of them it is possible to gratify the passions in due measure and, by doing so, to have them at our service for the purpose of education, having cured what was diseased in them. This objection, which gave to Aristotle a great handle for criticism, and to the defenders of these forms of poetry a starting-point for their arguments against Plato, we shall, in continuation of what we have already said, refute. . . . 50. 17–26. We shall agree, then, that the statesman must devise some outlets for these passions, but not so as to intensify our leanings towards them; on the contrary, so as to bridle them and keep the exercise of them within due limits; but these forms of poetry, which in addition to their garishness make an unmeasured appeal to these passions, are far from serving the purpose of purification; for purification depends not on excess but on restrained exercise, and has little likeness to the passions which it purifies.

IAMBL. *Myst.* I. 11 (Parthey). The powers of the human passions in us, hemmed in everywhere, wax stronger, but if they are permitted a modest exercise, within the limits of due proportion, they have a measured enjoyment and are satisfied, and being thereby purified they come to a stop in obedience to persuasion, and not to force. Therefore, both in comedy and in tragedy, by looking at the passions of others we stay our own passions, make them more moderate, and purify them.

Ibid. 3. 9. This is by no means to be called an elimination, or a purification and a cure; for it is innate in us not as a result of disease or superfluity or excess; it is divine.

6 (R^2 64, R^3 74)

MACR. 5. 18. 16. That it was the custom of the Aetolians to go to war with only one foot shod is shown by the famous tragic writer Euripides, in whose tragedy *Meleager* a messenger is introduced describing the dress of each of the captains who had come together to capture the boar. . . 19. In this matter . . . we shall not fail to point out a fact known to very few, that Euripides was criticized by Aristotle, who maintained that this was Euripides' ignorance; the Aetolians had not their left foot bare, but their right. That I may not make an assertion without proving it I will quote the very words of Aristotle in the second book[1] of his work *On Poets*, where he says this about Euripides: 'Euripides says the sons of Thestius went with their left foot unshod—"In their left step they were unshod of foot, while the right was shod—so that they should have one knee light". The custom of the Aetolians is just the opposite; their left foot is shod, the right unshod, I suppose because the leading foot should be light but not that which remains fixed.'

7 (R^2 65, R^3 75)

DIOG. LAERT. 2. 5. 46. Socrates had as rivals (so Aristotle says in the third book of his work on poetry) a certain Antilochus of Lemnos and Antiphon the soothsayer, as Pythagoras had Cylon of Croton; Homer while alive had Syagrus, and when dead Xenophanes of Colophon. Hesiod

[1] Reading in R. 79. 3 *secundum scripsit*, with Eyssenhardt.

when alive had Cecrops, and after death the aforesaid Xenophanes; Pindar had Amphimenes[1] of Cos, Thales had Pherecydes, Bias had Salarus of Priene, Pittacus had Antimenidas and Alcaeus, Anaxagoras had Sosibius, and Simonides had Timocreon.

8 (R² 66, R³ 76)

Ps.-Plu. *Vit. Hom.* 3–4. Aristotle in the third book of his work on poetry says that in the island of Ios, at the time when Neleus the son of Codrus ruled this Ionic colony, a certain girl who was a native of the island became pregnant by a spirit which was one of the companions of the Muses in the dance. When she saw the signs of her pregnancy she was ashamed of what had happened and betook herself to a place called Aegina. Pirates raided the place, captured the girl, and took her to Smyrna, which was then under the Lydians; this they did as a favour to Maeon, who was the king of Lydia and their friend. He fell in love with the girl for her beauty and married her. While she was living near the Meles the birth-pangs came upon her and she gave birth to Homer on the bank of the river. Maeon adopted him and brought him up as his own son, Critheis having died immediately after her delivery. Not long after, Maeon himself died. When the Lydians were being oppressed by the Aeolians and had decided to leave Smyrna, and their leaders had called on any who wished to follow them to leave the town, Homer (still an infant) said he too wished to follow; for which reason he was called Homer[2] instead of Melesigenes.

When he had grown up and already become famous for his poetry, he asked the god who were his ancestors and whence he came, and the god replied thus: 'Ios is thy mother's native island, which will receive thee dead; but beware of the riddle of young men.' . . . Not long after, while sailing to Thebes, to the festival of Kronos (this is a musical contest which they hold), he came to Ios. Here he sat on a rock and watched the fishermen sailing in, and asked them

[1] Reading in R. 79. 17 Ἀμφιμένης, with the MSS.
[2] ὁμηρεῖν—Ὅμηρος.

if they had anything. They had caught nothing, but were picking lice off themselves,[1] and owing to the difficulty of this chase they replied: 'What we caught we left; what we did not catch we bring with us', intimating that the lice they had caught they had killed and left behind, and those they had not caught they were carrying in their clothing. Homer failed to interpret the riddle and died of discouragement. The people of Ios buried him and inscribed on his tomb the high-sounding words: 'Here earth covers the sacred head, Homer, divine glorifier of heroes.'

Cf. GELL. 3. 11. 7 and *Homeri Opera*, ed. Allen, 5. 244, 247, 251–2.

Rose's fr. 77 is omitted, because it seems to belong not to the dialogue *On Poets*, but to the lost second book of the *Poetics*.

[1] Reading in R. 80. 22 φθειρίζεσθαι, with most of the MSS.

ON PHILOSOPHY

TESTIMONIA

PHILOD. *Piet.* 7^b4–8. . . . in the third book of Aristotle's work *On Philosophy.*

PRISC. LYDUS 41. 16–42. 3. Our materials have been taken and put together from Plato's *Timaeus* . . . and from Aristotle's *Physics, De Caelo, De Generatione et Corruptione,* and *Meteorologica,* and similarly from the *De Somno* and the *De Somniis,* and from what he wrote in dialogue form *On Philosophy* and *On the Worlds.*

SIMP. *in De Caelo* 288. 31–289. 2: see p. 5 *supra.*

ASCL. *in Metaph.* 112. 16–19. 'About the first principles' (Aristotle says) 'we have already spoken in the *Physics*'; and he promises to speak about these in Book α,[1] and to raise and solve the problems about them in the work *On Philosophy.*

1 (R² 4, R³ 1, W 1)

PLU. *Mor.* 1118 C. Of the inscriptions at Delphi that which was thought to be the most inspired was 'Know thyself'; it was this, as Aristotle has said in his Platonic works,[2] that induced in Socrates this mood of uncertainty and questioning.

2 (R² 3, R³ 2, W 2)

DIOG. LAERT. 2. 5. 23 (7). Aristotle says that Socrates went to Delphi; but also to the Isthmus, as Favorinus relates in the first book of his *Memoirs.*

3 (R² 5, R³ 3, W 3)

PORPH. apud STOB. 3. 21. 26. What and whose was the sacred injunction at Delphi, which bids him who is to seek anything

[1] Of the *Metaphysics.* [2] i.e. his dialogues.

from the god to know himself? . . . Whether it was Phemonoe . . . or Phanothea . . . or Bias or Thales or Chilon that set it up . . . or whether we should give credence rather to Clearchus, who says the injunction was that of the Pythian oracle and was given to Chilon when he inquired what it was best for men to learn; or whether even before the time of Chilon it was already inscribed in the temple that was founded after the temple of feathers[1] and that of bronze, as Aristotle has said in his work *On Philosophy* . . .

CLEM. AL. *Strom.* I. 14. 60. 3. The saying 'Know thyself' some have ascribed to Chilon, while Chameleon in his work on the gods ascribes it to Thales, and Aristotle ascribes it to the Pythian priestess.

4 (R² 6, R³ 4, W 4)

CLEM. AL. *Strom.* I. 14. 61. 1. Again, the saying 'Nothing in excess!' is ascribed to Chilon the Lacedaemonian. . . . 'Give a pledge, and ruin waits you' is cited by Cleomenes in his work on Hesiod. . . . The Aristotelian tradition ascribes it to Chilon, while Didymus assigns the advice to Thales.

5 (R² 7, R³ 5, W 5)

Etymol. Magn. 722. 16–17 (Sylburg) s.v. σοφιστής. Properly one who practises sophistry; but Aristotle uses it of the Seven Sages.

6 (R² 8, 29, R³ 6, 34, W 6)

DIOG. LAERT. I Prooem. 8 (6). Aristotle in the first book of his work *On Philosophy* says that the Magi are more ancient even than the Egyptians, and that according to them there are two first principles, a good spirit and an evil spirit, one called Zeus and Oromasdes, the other Hades and Areimanius.

PLINY, *N.H.* 30. 3. The art of magic undoubtedly began with Zoroaster in Persia, as the authorities agree. But it is not

[1] Cf. Paus. 10. 5. 9 'The second temple was made by bees out of wax and feathers.'

quite clear whether there was only one Zoroaster, or a later one as well. Eudoxus, who claimed it to be the most illustrious and most beneficial of the sects of philosophy, related that this Zoroaster lived six thousand years before the death of Plato; Aristotle agrees.

PLU. *Mor.* 370 C. Of the planets, which they call the gods of birth, the Chaldaeans describe two as beneficent, two as maleficent, the other three as intermediate and neutral. . . . Aristotle calls the one form, the other privation.

7 (R^2 9, R^3 7, W 7)

PHILOP. *in De An.* 186. 14–16. Aristotle says 'so-called' because the poems are thought not to be the work of Orpheus; Aristotle himself maintains this in the books *On Philosophy*; the opinions are those of Orpheus, but it is said[1] that Onomacritus spun them out in verse.

CIC. *N.D.* I. 38. 107. Aristotle says the poet Orpheus never existed; the Pythagoreans ascribe this Orphic poem to a certain Cercon.[2]

8 (R^2 2, R^3 13, W 8)

SYNES. *Calvit. Enc.* 22. 85 C. . . . if indeed a proverb is a wise thing; and why should those things not be wise which Aristotle describes as relics, saved by their conciseness and cleverness when ancient philosophy perished in the widespread destruction of mankind?

PHILOPONUS *in Nicom. Isagogen* I. I. Wisdom (*σοφία*) was so called as being a sort of clearness (*σάφεια*), inasmuch as it makes all things clear. This clearness, being, as it were, something light (*φαές*), has acquired its name from that of light (*φάος, φῶς*), because it brings hidden things to light. Since, then, as Aristotle says, things intelligible and divine, even if they are most clear in their own nature, seem to us dark

[1] Reading in R. 26. 19 *φασιν*, with Hayduck.
[2] Reading in R. 26. 22 *Cerconis*, with the MSS.

and dim because of the mist of the body which hangs over us, men naturally gave to the knowledge which brings these things into the light for us the name of wisdom. But since we use the words 'wisdom' and 'wise' in a general way, it must be realized that these words are ambiguous. They have been taken by the ancients in five ways, which Aristotle mentions in his ten books *On Philosophy*. For you must know that men perish in diverse ways—both by plagues and famines and earthquakes and wars and various diseases and by other causes, but above all by more violent cataclysms, such as that in the time of Deucalion is said to have been; it was a great cataclysm but not the greatest of all. For herdsmen and those who have their occupation in the mountains or the foothills are saved, while the plains and the dwellers in them are engulfed; so, at least, they say that Dardanus was swept by the flood from Samothrace to what was afterwards called Troy, and thus was saved. Those who are saved from the water must live on the uplands, as the poet shows when he says: 'First Zeus the cloud-gatherer begat Dardanus, and he stablished Dardania, for not yet was holy Ilios built upon the plain to be a city of mortal men, but still they dwelt on slopes of many-fountained Ida.[1] The word 'still' shows that they had not yet courage to live in the plains. These survivors, then, not having the means of sustenance, were forced by necessity to think of useful devices—the grinding of corn, sowing, and the like—and they gave the name of wisdom to such thought, thought which discovered what was useful with a view to the necessities of life, and the name of wise to anyone who had had such thoughts. Again, they devised arts, as the poet says, 'at the prompting of Athene'—arts not limited to the necessities of life, but going on to the production of beauty and elegance; and this again men have called wisdom, and its discoverer wise, as in the phrase 'A wise craftsman framed it',[2] 'knowing well by Athene's promptings of wisdom'.[3] For, because of the excellence of the discoveries, they ascribed the thought of these things to God. Again, they turned their attention to politics, and invented

[1] Hom. *Il.* 20. 215–18. [2] Cf. ibid. 23. 712.
[3] Cf. ibid. 15. 412, *Od.* 16. 233.

laws, and all the things that hold a state together; and such thought also they called wisdom; for such were the Seven Wise Men—men who attained political virtues. Then they went farther and proceeded to bodies themselves and the nature that fashions them, and this they called by the special name of natural science, and its possessors we describe as wise in the affairs of nature. Fifthly, men applied the name in connexion with things divine, supramundane, and completely unchangeable, and called the knowledge of these things the highest wisdom.

9 (W 9)

SEXT. EMP. *Phys.* 2. 45–46. Some say that movement exists, others deny this . . . namely the followers of Parmenides and Melissus, whom Aristotle has called immobilists[1] and non-physical thinkers—immobilists because they maintain the immobility of being, non-physical because nature is the source of movement, and in saying that nothing moves they denied the existence of nature.

10 (R² 10, R³ 8, W 10)

PROCL. apud PHILOP. *De Aet. Mundi*, p. 31. 17 (Rabe). It looks as though there were nothing in Plato that Aristotle rejected so firmly as the theory of Ideas, not only in his logical writings . . . 20 but also in his ethical writings . . . 21 and in his physical writings . . . 32. 1 and much more in his *Metaphysics* . . . 5–8 and in his dialogues, where he asseverates most clearly that he cannot agree with this doctrine, even if he lays himself open to the charge of opposing it from love of polemic.

PLU. *Mor.* 1115 b–c: see p. 4 *supra*.

11 (R² 11, R³ 9, W 11)

SYRIAN. *in Metaph.* 159. 33–160. 5. Aristotle himself admits that he has said nothing against the hypotheses of the

[1] Omitting τῆς φύσεως, with some MSS. This seems to be a punning use of the word στασιώτης.

Platonists and quite fails to keep pace with the doctrine of the ideal numbers, if these are different from the mathematical. This is shown by the words in the second book of the work *On Philosophy*: 'Thus if the Ideas are a different sort of number, not mathematical number, we can have no understanding of it; for of the majority of us, at all events, who comprehends any other number?' Thus in fact he has addressed his refutation to the multitude who know no number other than that which is composed of units, and did not begin to grasp the thought of these divine thinkers.

ALEX. APH. *in Metaph.* 117. 23–118. 1. Aristotle sets out the Platonic dogma, which he has also stated in the work *On Philosophy*. Wishing to reduce realities (which is what he always means by 'substances') to the first principles which they assumed (the great and the small, which they called the indefinite dyad), they said the first principles of length were the short and long (the assumption being that length takes its origin from a long and short, i.e. from a great and small, or that every line falls under one or other of these), and that the first principles of the plane were the narrow and wide, which are themselves also great and small.

ARIST. *De An.* 404b16–24. In the same way Plato, in the *Timaeus*, fashions the soul out of his elements; for like, he holds, is known by like, and things are formed out of the principles or elements.[1] Similarly also in the work *On Philosophy* it was set forth that the Animal itself is compounded of the Idea itself of the One together with the primary length, breadth, and depth, everything else[2] being similarly constituted. Again, he puts his view in yet other terms: Mind is the monad, knowledge the dyad (because it goes undeviatingly from one point to another), opinion the number of the plane, sensation the number of the solid.

SIMP. *in De An.* 28. 7–9. Aristotle now applies the name *On Philosophy* to his work *On the Good* (taken down from plato's

[1] sc. so that the soul must be so too.
[2] sc. the objects of its cognition.

lectures), in which he relates both the Pythagorean opinions about reality and those of Plato.

Cf. PHILOP. *in De An.* 75. 34–76. 1 (see p. 116 *infra*).

PS.-ALEX. *in Metaph.* 777. 16–21. The principle of the One they did not all introduce in the same way. Some said that the numbers themselves introduced the Forms into spatial magnitudes, the number 2 doing so for the line, the number 3 for the plane, the number 4 for the solid (Aristotle relates this about Plato in the work *On Philosophy*, and that is why he here summarizes only briefly and concisely the theory of the Platonists); while others explained the form of the spatial magnitudes by participation in the One.

12 *a* (R² 12, R³ 10, W 12*a*)

SEXT. EMP. *Phys.* I. 20–23. Aristotle used to say that men's thought of gods sprang from two sources—the experiences of the soul, and the phenomena of the heavens. To the first head belonged the inspiration and prophetic power of the soul in dreams. For when (he says) the soul is isolated in sleep, it assumes its true nature and foresees and foretells the future. So is it too with the soul, when at death it is severed from the body. At all events, Aristotle accepts even Homer as having observed this; for Homer has represented Patroclus, in the moment of his death, as foretelling the death of Hector, and Hector as foretelling the end of Achilles. It was from such events (he says) that men came to suspect the existence of something divine,[1] of that which is in its nature akin to the soul and of all things most full of knowledge. But the heavenly bodies also contributed to this belief; seeing by day the sun running his circular course, and by night the well-ordered movement of the other stars, they came to think that there is a God who is the cause of such movement and order. Such was the belief of Aristotle.

CIC. *Div. ad Brut.* I. 30. 63. When, therefore, sleep has freed the mind from the society and contact of the body, then it

[1] Reading in R. 28. 13 θεῖον, with Mutschmann.

remembers the past, discerns the present, and foresees the future; for the body of a sleeper lies like that of a dead man, but his mind is active and alive . . . and so when death approaches it is much more divine. . . . 64. That dying men have foreknowledge Posidonius confirms by the example he adduces. . . . Another instance of this is Homer's Hector, who when dying announces the approaching death of Achilles.

12 *b* (R² 13, R³ 11, W 12 *b*)

SEXT. EMP. *Math.* 9 (*Phys.* 1) 26–27. Some men, when they come to the unswerving and well-ordered movement of the heavenly bodies, say that in this the thought of gods had its origin; for as, if one had sat on the Trojan Mount Ida and seen the array of the Greeks approaching the plains in good order and arrangement, 'horsemen first with horses and chariots, and footmen behind',[1] such a one would certainly have come to think that there was someone arranging such an array and commanding the soldiers ranged under him, Nestor or some other hero who knew 'how to order horses and bucklered warriors'.[2] And as one familiar with ships, as soon as he sees from afar a ship running before the wind with all its sails well set, knows that there is someone directing it and steering it[3] to its appointed harbours, so those who first looked up to heaven and saw the sun running its race from its rising to its setting, and the orderly dances of the stars, looked for the Craftsman of this lovely design, and surmised that it came about not by chance but by the agency of some mightier and imperishable nature, which was God.

13 (R² 14, R³ 12, W 13)

CIC. *N.D.* 2. 37. 95–96. Great was the saying of Aristotle: 'Suppose there were men who had lived always underground, in good and well-lighted dwellings, adorned with statues and pictures, and furnished with everything in which those who are thought happy abound. Suppose, however, that they had

[1] Hom. *Il.* 4. 297. [2] Ibid. 2. 554.
[3] Reading in R. 29. 6 κατάγων, with Mutschmann.

never gone above ground, but had learned by report and hearsay that there is a divine authority and power. Suppose that then, at some time, the jaws of the earth opened, and they were able to escape and make their way from those hidden dwellings into these regions which we inhabit. When they suddenly saw earth and seas and sky, when they learned the grandeur of clouds and the power of winds, when they saw the sun and learned his grandeur and beauty and the power shown in his filling the sky with light and making day; when, again, night darkened the lands and they saw the whole sky picked out and adorned with stars, and the varying lights of the moon as it waxes and wanes, and the risings and settings of all these bodies, and their courses settled and immutable to all eternity; when they saw those things, most certainly they would have judged both that there are gods and that these great works are the works of gods.' Thus far Aristotle.

PHILO, *Leg. Alleg*. 3. 32. 97–99. The earliest thinkers inquired how we came to recognize the divine. Later, the most highly esteemed philosophers said that it was from the world and its parts and the powers inherent in these that we came to grasp their cause. If one saw a house carefully furnished with entrances, colonnades, men's quarters, women's quarters, and all the other buildings, he would acquire an idea of the architect, since he would reflect that the house could not have been completed without the art of a craftsman; and so too with a city, a ship, or any structure small or great. So also if one comes into this world as into a vast house or city, and sees the heavens revolving in a circle and containing all things within them, planets and unwandering stars moving uniformly in orderly and harmonious fashion for the good of the whole, earth occupying the midmost region, streams of water and air in between, living things also, mortal and immortal, varieties of plants and crops; he will surely reason that these things have not been framed without perfect skill, but that there both was and is a framer of this universe—God. Those, then, who reason thus grasp God by way of his shadow, apprehending the Craftsman through his works.

Cf. PHILO, *De Praem. et Poen.* 7. 40–46, *De Spec. Leg.* I. 35. 185–36. 194.

14 (R² 44, R³ 14, W 14)

SEN. *Q.N.* 7. 30. Aristotle says excellently that we should nowhere be more modest than in matters of religion. If we compose ourselves before we enter temples . . . how much more should we do this when we discuss the constellations, the stars, and the nature of the gods,[1] to guard against saying anything rashly and imprudently, either not knowing it to be true or knowing it to be false!

Cf. PLU. *Mor.* 477 c–f.

15 (R² 45, R³ 15, W 15)

SYNESIUS, *Dio.* 10. 48 a. . . . as Aristotle claims that those who are being initiated into the mysteries are to be expected not to learn anything but to suffer some change, to be put into a certain condition, i.e. to be fitted for some purpose.

MICHAEL PSELLUS, *Schol. ad Joh. Climacum* (*Cat. des Man. Alch. Grecs*, ed. Bidez, 1928), 6. 171. I undertook to teach you what I have learned, not what I have experienced . . . the one is matter for teaching, the other for mystical experience. The first comes to men by hearing, the second comes when reason itself has experienced illumination—which Aristotle described as mysterious and akin to the Eleusinian rites (for in these he who was initiated into the mysteries was being moulded, not being taught).

16 (R² 15, R³ 16, W 16)

SIMP. *in De Caelo* 289. 1–15. Aristotle speaks of this in the work *On Philosophy*. In general, where there is a better there is a best. Since, then, among existing things one is better than another, there is also something that is best, which will

[1] Reading in R. 31. 7–8 *de sideribus, de stellis, de deorum natura disputamus*, with Gercke.

be the divine. Now that which changes is changed either by something else or by itself, and if by something else, either by something better or by something worse, and if by itself, either to something worse or through desire for something better; but the divine has nothing better than itself by which it may be changed (for that other would then have been more divine), nor on the other hand is it lawful for the better to be affected by the worse; besides, if it were changed by something worse, it would have admitted some evil into itself, but nothing in it is evil. On the other hand, it does not change itself through desire for something better, since it lacks none of its own excellences; nor again does it change itself for the worse, since even a man does not willingly make himself worse, nor has it anything evil such as it would have acquired from a change to the worse. This proof, too, Aristotle took over from the second book of Plato's *Republic*.

17 (R² 16, R³ 17, W 17)

Schol. in Proverb. Salomonis, cod. Paris. gr. 174, f. 46 *a*. To Aristotle belongs the following: 'There is either one first principle or many. If there is one, we have what we are looking for; if there are many, they are either ordered or disordered. Now if they are disordered, their products are more so, and the world is not a world but a chaos; besides, that which is contrary to nature belongs to that which is by nature non-existent. If on the other hand they are ordered, they were ordered either by themselves or by some outside cause. But if they were ordered by themselves, they have something common that unites them, and that is the first principle.'

18 (R² 17, R³ 18, W 18)

PHILO, *De Aet. Mundi* 3. 10–11. Aristotle was surely speaking piously and devoutly when he insisted that the world is ungenerated and imperishable, and convicted of grave ungodliness those who maintained the opposite, who thought that the great visible god, which contains in truth sun and moon and the remaining pantheon of planets and unwandering stars, is no better than the work of man's hands; he used to say in mockery (we are told) that in the past he had feared lest his house be destroyed by violent winds or storms beyond the ordinary, or by time or by lack of proper maintenance, but that now a greater danger hung over him, from those who by argument destroyed the whole world.

19 *a* (R³ 19, W 19 *a*)

PHILO, *De Act. Mundi* 5. 20–24 .The arguments which prove the world to be ungenerated and imperishable should, out of respect for the visible god, be given their proper precedence and placed earlier in the discussion. To all things that admit of being destroyed there are ordained two causes of destruction, one inward, the other outward. Iron, bronze, and suchlike substances you will find being destroyed from within when rust invades and devours them like a creeping disease, and from without when a house or a city is set on fire and they catch fire from it and are destroyed by the fierce rush of flame; and similarly death comes to living beings from themselves when they fall sick, and from outside when they have their throats cut or are stoned or burned to death or suffer the unclean death by hanging. If the world, too, is destroyed, it must be either by something outside or by one of the powers in itself. Now each of these is impossible. For there is nothing outside the world, since all things have contributed to its completeness. For so will it be one, whole, and ageless; one because only if something had been left out of its composition would there be another world like the present world; whole because the whole of being has been expended on it; ageless and diseaseless because bodies caught by disease and old age are destroyed by the violent assault from without of heat and cold and the other contrary forces, of which none can escape and circle round and attack the world, since all without exception are entirely enclosed within it. If there *is* anything outside, it must be a complete void or an impassive nature which cannot suffer or do anything. Nor again will the world be destroyed by anything within it—firstly because the part would then be both greater and more powerful than the whole, which is the most incredible of all things; for the world, wielding unsurpassable power, directs all its parts and is directed by none; secondly because, there being two causes of destruction, one within and one without, things that can suffer the one are necessarily susceptible also to the other. The evidence? Ox and horse and man and such-like animals, because they can be destroyed by iron, will also perish by disease. For it is hard, nay impossible, to find anything that is fitted to be subject to the external cause of destruction and entirely insusceptible to the internal. Since, then, it was shown that the world will not be destroyed by anything without, because absolutely nothing has been left outside, neither will it be destroyed by anything within, because of the preceding argument to the effect that that which is susceptible to the one cause is also susceptible to the other.

19 *b* (R[3] 20, W 19 *b*)

PHILO, *De Aet. Mundi* 6. 28—7. 34. This may be put in another way. Of composite bodies all that are destroyed are dissolved into their components; but dissolution is surely nothing but reduction to the natural state of the parts, so that conversely where there is composition, it has forced into an unnatural state the parts that have come together. And indeed it seems to be so beyond a doubt. For we men were put together by borrowing little parts of the four elements, which belong in their entirety to the whole universe—earth, water, air, and fire. Now these parts when mixed are robbed of their natural position, the upward-travelling heat being forced down,[1] the earthy and heavy substance being made light and seizing in turn the upper region, which is occupied by the earthiest of our parts, the head. The worst of bonds is that which is fastened by violence; this is violent and shortlived, for it is broken sooner by those who have been bound, because they shake off the noose through longing for their natural movement, to which they hasten. For, as the tragic poet says, 'Things born of earth return to earth,

[1] Reading in R. 35. 13–14 κατωσθείσης, with Diels.

things born of an ethereal seed return to the pole of heaven; nothing that comes into being dies; one departs in one direction, one in another,[1] and each shows its own form.'[2] For all things that perish, then, this is the law and this the rule prescribed—when the parts that have come together in the mixture have settled down they must in place of their natural order have experienced disorder, and must move to the opposites of their natural places, so that they seem to be in a sense exiles, but when they are separated they turn back to their natural sphere. Now the world has no part in the disorder we have spoken of; for let us consider. If the world is perishing, its parts must now each be placed in the region unnatural to it. But this we cannot easily suppose; for to all the parts of the world have fallen perfect position and harmonious arrangement, so that each, as though fond of its own country, seeks no change to a better. For this reason, then, was assigned to earth the midmost position, to which[3] all earthy things, even if you throw them up, descend. This is an indication of their natural place; for in that region in which a thing brought thither stays and rests, when under no compulsion, there it has its home. Secondly, water is spread over the earth, and air and fire have moved from the middle to the upper region, to air falling the region between water and fire, and to fire the highest region of all. And so, even if you light a torch and throw it to the ground, the flame will none the less strive against you and lighten itself and return to the natural motion of fire. If, then, the cause of destruction of other creatures is their unnatural situation,[4] but in the world each of its parts is situated according to nature and has had its proper place assigned to it, the world may justly be called imperishable.

19 *c* (R³ 21, W 19 *c*)

PHILO, *De Aet. Mundi* 8. 39–43. The most conclusive argument is that on which I know very many people to pride themselves, as on something most precise and quite irrefutable.

[1] Reading in R. 35. 23 πρὸς ἄλλο, with the MSS.

[2] Eur. fr. 836 Nauck.

[3] Reading in R. 36. 11 ἐφ' ὅν.

[4] Reading in R. 36. 20–1 ἡ παρὰ φύσιν τάξις τῶν ἄλλων, with Cohn.

They ask, Why should God destroy the world?[1] Either to save himself from continuing in world-making, or in order to make another world. The former of these purposes is alien to God; for what befits him is to turn disorder into order, not order into disorder; and further, he would be admitting into himself repentance, an affection and disease of the soul. For he should either not have made a world at all, or else, if he judged the work becoming to him, should have rejoiced in the product. The second alternative deserves full examination. For if instead of the present world he is to make another, the world he makes will be in any case either worse or better than the present world, or like to it, and each of these possibilities is open to objection. (1) If it is worse, its artificer will be worse; but the works of God are blameless, exempt from criticism, incapable of improvement, fashioned as they are by the most perfect art and knowledge. For, as the saying goes, 'not even a woman is so lacking in good judgement as to prefer the worse[2] when the better is available';[3] and it is befitting for God to give shape to the shapeless and to deck the ugliest things with marvellous beauties. (2) If the new world is like the old, its artificer will have laboured in vain, differing in nothing from mere children, who often, when they make sand-castles on the shore, build them up and then pull them down. It were far better, instead of making a new world like the old, neither to take away nor to add anything, nor change anything for better or for worse, but to leave the original world in its place. (3) If he is to make a better world, the artificer himself must become better, so that when he made the former world he must have been more imperfect both in art and in wisdom—which it is not lawful even to suspect. For God is equal and like to himself, admitting neither slackening towards the worse nor intensification towards the better.

20 (R² 18, R³ 22, W 20)

CIC. *Lucullus* 38. 119 (Plasberg). When your wise Stoic has

[1] Reading in R. 36. 27 *φθερεῖ*, with Gomperz.
[2] Reading in R. 37. 12 *χερείον'*, with Meineke.
[3] Reading in R. 37. 13 *ἀμεινοτέρων παρεόντων*, with Mangey.

said all these things to you syllable by syllable, Aristotle will come with the golden flow of his speech, to say that the Stoic is talking nonsense; he will say that the world never came into being, because there never was a new design from which so noble a work could have taken its beginning, and that it is so well designed in every part that no force can effect such great movements and so great a change, no old age can come upon the world by lapse of time, so that this beauteous world should ever fall to pieces and perish.

LACT. *Inst.* 2. 10. 24. If the world can perish as a whole because it perishes in parts, it clearly has at some time come into being; and as fragility proclaims a beginning, so it proclaims an end. If that is true, Aristotle could not save the world itself from having a beginning. Now if Plato and Epicurus wring this admission from Aristotle, then in spite of the eloquence of Plato and Aristotle, who thought the world would last for ever, Epicurus will force from them the same unwilling conclusion, since it follows that the world has also an end.

21 (R² 19–20, R³ 23–24, W 21)

CIC. *N.D.* 2. 15. 42. Since some living things have their origin in earth, others in water, others in air, Aristotle thinks it absurd to suppose that in that part which is fittest to generate living things no animal should be born. Now the stars occupy the ethereal region; and since that region is the least dense and is always in movement and activity, the animal born in it must have the keenest perception and the swiftest movement. Thus, since it is in ether that the stars are born, it is proper that in these there should be perception and intelligence. From which it follows that the stars must be reckoned among the gods.

Ibid. 16. 44. Aristotle is to be praised, too, for judging that all things that move do so either by nature or by compulsion or by choice, and that the sun and moon and all the stars are in movement, and that things that move by nature move either downwards by virtue of weight or upwards by virtue of lightness, neither of which could happen to the stars, because their movement is in an orb or circle. Nor again can it be said that some greater force makes the stars move contrary to nature; for what power can be greater? What remains, then, is that the movement of the stars is voluntary. He who sees these things would be acting not only ignorantly but also impiously if he denied that there are gods.

22 (W 22)

STOB. I. 43 = *Dox. Gr.* 432. 4–8. Plato and Aristotle say there are four kinds of animals—of land, of water, winged, heavenly. For the stars too, they say, are said to be animals, and the world itself is divine,[1] a reasonable immortal animal.

OLYMP. *in Phd.* 180. 22–23 (Norvin). Aristotle ascribes the whole process of creation to the heavenly animals.[2]

NEMES. *De Nat. Hom.* ch. 34. Aristotle ascribes the generation of these to the sun and the zodiacal circle.

Cf. PLU. *Mor.* 908 f, PS.-GALEN, *Phil. Hist.* ch. 35.

23 (R[2] 37, R[3] 42, W 23)

OLYMP. *in Phd.* 200. 3–6 (Norvin). That there must even be a whole race of men which is thus nourished is shown by the case of the man in these parts who was nourished by the sun's rays alone; Aristotle told about him, having himself seen him.

Ibid. 239. 19–21. If Aristotle recorded the case of a man in this world who was sleepless and was nourished only by the sun's rays, what must we think of things in another world?

24 (R[2] 39, R[3] 48, W 24)

OLYMP. *in Phd.* 26. 22–27. 4 (Norvin). Proclus would have heavenly bodies possess only sight and hearing, as Aristotle

[1] Reading λέγεσθαι καὶ τὸν κόσμον καὐτὸν ἔνθεον, with Diels.
[2] i.e. to the zodiacal animals.

also would; of the senses they have only these, which are those that contribute to well-being, not those that contribute to being, as the other senses do. The poet testifies to this, saying: 'Sun, who seest all things and hearest all things'[1]—which implies that the heavenly bodies have only sight and hearing. Aristotle adds that these senses, most of all, have knowledge by way of activity rather than of passivity, and are fitter for the unchanging heavenly bodies. Damascius, however, holds that these bodies have also the other senses.

25 (R² 43, R³ 47, W 25)

PLU. *Mor.* 1138 c–1104 b. We have shown that Plato rejected the other forms of music not from ignorance or musical inexperience but as being unbefitting to such a constitution; we will next show that he was skilled in music. . . . 1139 b–1140 b. On the theme that music is something noble, divine, and grand, Aristotle, the pupil of Plato, says: 'Music is heavenly, by nature divine, beautiful, and inspired; having by nature four parts, it has two means, the arithmetical and the harmonic, and the parts of it, their extents, and their excesses one over another, have numerical and proportionate relations; for tunes[2] are arranged in two tetrachords.[3] These are his words. He meant that the body of music was composed of unlike parts; which, however, harmonized with each other. But its means also harmonized in arithmetical ratio; for the highest note, proportioned to the lowest in the ratio of 2 : 1, completed the octave. For music has, as we said before, a highest note of twelve units and a lowest note of six. Paramese, harmonizing with hypate in the ratio of 3 : 2, has nine units, while, as we said, mese has eight.[4] It is of these that the fundamental musical intervals are composed—the fourth,

[1] Hom. *Il.* 3. 277, *Od.* 12. 323.

[2] Reading in R. 53. 7 μέλη, with the MSS.

[3] The Greeks regarded a musical scale as formed by two tetrachords, either so that the highest note of one was identical with the lowest note of the other (as in EFGAB♭CD), or so that there was an interval of a note between them (as in EFGA BCDE).

[4] Plutarch takes account only of the fundamental notes of the scale—the base note (hypate), the fourth (mese), the fifth (paramese), and the octave (neate).

involving the ratio 4 : 3, the fifth, involving the ratio 3 : 2, and the octave, involving the ratio 2 : 1. But the ratio 9 : 8 is also found, which gives the interval of a single tone. The notes of the scale exceed, and are exceeded by, the notes, and the intervals by the intervals, by the same excesses, both in geometrical progression and in arithmetical. Aristotle, then, describes them as having such values, neate exceeding mese by the third part of itself,[1] hypate exceeded by paramese in the same ratio,[2] so that the excesses are correlative; the notes exceed and are exceeded by the same fractions. Thus the extreme notes respectively exceed and are exceeded by mese and paramese in the same ratios, 4 : 3 and 3 : 2.[3] Such an excess is the harmonic.[4] And neate exceeds mese and paramese exceeds hypate by arithmetically equal fractions.[5] For paramese is to mese as 9 : 8, neate to hypate as 2 : 1, paramese to hypate as 3 : 2, and mese to hypate as 4 : 3. Thus, according to Aristotle, is the scale constituted in respect of the notes and the corresponding numbers.

Both it and all its notes are, as regards their inmost nature, constituted by the even, the odd,[6] and the even-odd. For it is itself, as a whole, even, involving four terms, while its parts and their ratios are even, odd, and even-odd; neate is even, containing twelve units, paramese odd, containing nine, mese even, containing eight, hypate even-odd, containing six.[7] Being itself thus constituted, and its notes so related

[1] Reading in R. 53. 27 *αὐτῆς*, with Bernardakis.

[2] i.e. by the third part of paramese.

[3] i.e. neate : mese = paramese : hypate = 3 : 2, and neate : paramese = mese : hypate = 4 : 3.

[4] Three quantities a, b, c were described by the Greeks as forming a harmonic progression if $a = b + \frac{a}{n}$ and $b = c + \frac{c}{n}$. $12 = 8 + \frac{12}{3}$ and $8 = 6 + \frac{6}{3}$, so that 12, 8, 6 (neate, mese, hypate) formed a harmonic progression.

[5] This sentence cannot be right as it stands in the Greek; the sense requires in R. 54. 2–4 something like *ἡ δὲ νεάτη ὑπερέχει τῆς μέσης κατ' ἀριθμητικὸν λόγον ἴσῳ μέρει καὶ ἡ παραμέση τῆς ὑπάτης.* Neate, paramese, mese, and hypate being to one another as 12, 9, 8, 6, neate exceeds mese, and paramese exceeds hypate, by equal fractions, i.e. by a half.

[6] The context seems to demand in R. 54. 9–10 the reading *ἔκ τε τῆς ἀρτίας καὶ περισσῆς*, which was proposed by Volkmann.

[7] 12 is said to be even but 6 to be even-odd, because 'even-odd' was applied, and confined, to numbers whose halves are odd.

in respect of their mutual excesses and ratios, it is as a whole in harmony with itself and with its parts. But furthermore, of the senses that come into being in bodies, those which are heavenly and divine, affording by God's help and by reason of this harmony[1] perception to men—namely sight and hearing—exhibit harmony by the aid of sound and light. And the senses that accompany them are, *qua* senses, harmoniously constituted; for it is not without harmony that these too produce their effects; they are lesser than sight and hearing, but not derived from them. When God is present, those two come into being in bodies, in accordance with numerical principles, and their nature is both powerful and beautiful.

It is clear, then, that the ancient Greeks were right in valuing musical education most highly of all.

26 (R^2 21, R^3 26, W 26)

Cic. *N.D.* I. 13. 33 (speaking in the person of an Epicurean). 'Aristotle, in the third book of his work *On Philosophy*, creates much confusion through dissenting[2] from his master Plato. For now he ascribes all divinity to mind, now he says the world itself is a god, now he sets another god over the world and ascribes to him the rôle of ruling and preserving the movement of the world by a sort of backward rotation. Then he says the heat of the heavens is a god, not realizing that the heavens are part of the world, which he has himself elsewhere called a god. But how can the divine sense-perception which he ascribes to the heavens be preserved in a movement so speedy? Where, again, are all the gods of popular belief, if we count the heavens, too, as a god? And when he himself demands that God be without a body, he deprives him of all sense-perception, and even of foresight. Moreover, how can the world move[3] if it lacks body, and how, if it is always moving itself, can it be calm and blessed?'

[1] Reading διὰ τὴν ἁρμονίαν (with the MSS.) after αἴσθησιν in R. 54. 21, instead of in R. 54. 20.

[2] Omitting *non* in R. 39. 19, with the MSS.

[3] Reading in R. 40. 2 *modo mundus moveri*, with the MSS.

27 (W 27)

Cic. *Acad.* I. 7. 26. Therefore air—this word[1] too we use as a Latin word—and fire and water and earth are primary; from them spring the forms of animals and of the fruits of the earth. Therefore these are called first principles and, to translate from the Greek, elements; of them, air and fire have the power of producing movement and causing change, while the part of the others—water and earth—is to receive and, as it were, to suffer. The fifth kind, from which were derived stars and minds, Aristotle thought to be something distinct, and unlike the four I have mentioned above.

Cic. *Tusc.* I. 10. 22. Aristotle, who far exceeded all others—Plato I always except—both in intellect and in industry, after taking account of the four well-known classes of first principles from which all things were derived, considers that there is a fifth kind of thing, from which comes mind; for thought, foresight, learning and teaching, discovery, the riches of memory, love and hate, desire and fear, distress and joy, these and their like (he thinks) cannot be included in any of the four classes; he adds a fifth, nameless class, and so calls the mind itself by the new name ἐνδελέχεια, as being a continuous and endless movement.

Ibid. I. 17. 41. If the mind is either a certain number (a subtle but not a very clear hypothesis) or the fifth nature, which is unnamed but well understood, these beings are much more perfect and pure, so that they move very far from the earth.

Ibid. I. 26. 65–27. 66. But if there is a fifth nature, introduced first[2] by Aristotle, this is the nature both of gods and of minds.[3] We, following this opinion, have expressed it in these very words in our *Consolatio*: 'The origin of minds is not to be found on earth; for in minds there is nothing mixed and composite, nothing that seems to be born and fashioned of earth, nothing even resembling water, air, or fire. For in

[1] sc. *aer.* [2] Reading *inducta primum, haec,* with the MSS.
[3] Reading *animorum,* with the MSS.

these natures there is nothing that has the power of memory, mind, and thought, that retains the past, foresees the future, and can grasp the present—which alone are living powers—nor will it ever be discovered whence these can come to man, except from God.' There is, therefore, a singular nature and power of mind, disjoined from these customary and well-known natures. Thus, whatever it is that feels, knows, lives, thrives, it must be celestial and divine, and therefore eternal. Nor can the God whom we know be otherwise understood than as a mind apart and free, separated from all mortal admixture, feeding and moving all things, and itself endowed with eternal motion. Of this kind and of the same nature is the human mind.

CLEM. ROM. *Recogn.* 8. 15. Aristotle introduced a fifth element, which he called *ἀκατονόμαστον*, i.e. unnameable, doubtless pointing to the being who by uniting the four elements in one made the world.

28 (W 30)

ARIST. *Phys.* 194ᵃ27–36. The end and the means must be studied by the same science; and the nature is the end (for the terminus of a continuous process is also its final cause;[1] hence the poet's[2] absurd remark, 'He has the end for which he was born',[3] which is absurd because not every final point but only that which is best is a final cause). Indeed, some arts *make* their matter and others make it workable, and we use their matter as existing for our own sake (for we are the end, in one of the two senses we have distinguished in the work *On Philosophy*).

[1] Reading ἔστι τι τέλος, τοῦτο τὸ ἔσχατον καὶ τὸ οὗ ἕνεκα.

[2] An unidentified comic poet (Kock, *Com. Att. Fr.* iii, p. 493).

[3] i.e. death.

ON JUSTICE

TESTIMONIUM

CIC. *Rep*. 3. 8. 12. The other writer[1] filled four huge books with his views on justice itself.

1 (R² 71, R³ 82)

DEMETR. *Eloc*. 28. Neither in passages meant to rouse terror, then, as I have shown, nor in passages of pathos or moral reflection, is the use of words of similar ending serviceable; for pathos wants to be simple and unforced, and so does moral reflection. At all events in Aristotle's work *On Justice*, if the speaker who is bewailing the fate of Athens were to say 'They took an enemy city and lost their own; compare their gain with their loss', he would have used the language of pathos and pity; but if he uses the jingle 'They took an enemy city and lost their own; compare the profit they gained with the loss they sustained', by heaven he will rouse not sympathy nor pity[2] but (as we say) smiles mixed with tears. To use such false artifices in pathetic passages is, in proverbial language, to play among those who mourn.

2 (R² 73, R³ 84)

SUET. *De Blasph*. p. 416 (Miller) s.v. *Εὐρύβατος*. A criminal, also called Eurybates. . . . Aristotle in the first book of his work *On Justice* says he was a thief who when he was caught and put in chains and encouraged by the warders to show how he got over walls and into houses, 'on being set free, fastened spikes to his feet and took the sponges, climbed very easily, escaped from the roof, and got away'.

Cf. GREG. COR. *Ad Hermog*. c. 19, and SUIDAS s.v. *Εὐρύβατος*.

[1] Aristotle.

[2] Reading in R. 87. 1 *κινήσει οὐδὲ ἔλεον ἀλλά*, with the MSS.

3 (R^2 74, R^3 85)

LACT. *Inst.* 5. 15. Carneades,[1] in order to refute Aristotle's and Plato's praise of justice, in his first discourse collected all the things that used to be said in favour of justice, with the object of disproving them, as he in fact did.

LACT. *Epit.* 55. A great number of philosophers, but principally Plato and Aristotle, said much about justice, defending it and bestowing the highest praise on it because it assigns to each man what is his own and preserves equity in all things, and maintained that while the other virtues are, so to speak, silent and inward, it is justice alone that is not so self-contained and hidden, but stands boldly forth in readiness to act well for the general good.

4 (R^2 75, R^3 86)

PLU. *Mor.* 1040 e. Chrysippus says in criticism of Aristotle on the subject of justice that he is not right in saying that if pleasure is the end justice is destroyed, and with justice each of the other virtues.

Cf. CIC. *Hortensius*, fr. 81 (Müller) = AUGUST. *C. Iul. Pel.* 4. 14. 72.

5 (R^2 76, R^3 87)

PORPH. *in De Int.* apud BOETH. *in De Int.* ed. 2, 1. 1, p. 27 (Meiser). Aristotle in his work *On Justice* says 'thoughts and sensations are from the very start distinct in their nature'.

6 (R^3 88)

THEM. *Or.* 26 d–27 b. Zeno, the founder of the Stoic school, though he was in all other respects proud and lofty, yet was pleased and flattered when on the strength of his discourses the Athenians conferred citizenship on him, a stranger and

[1] In Cicero's *De Re Publica*.

a Phoenician; is it likely then that I was so boorish, and so heedless of Aristotle, whom I had taken as my master both in life and in philosophy, as to think all honour, no matter from whom or on what ground, a thankless and mercenary object for a good man? Do I not remember the grounds on which Aristotle distinguishes vanity from true pride? In distinguishing them,[1] he says somewhere that with regard to great honours, as with regard to all other things that are called good, there is an immoderate care for them, but also a moderate and reasonable care. He adds that the man who is puffed up and raises his eyebrows at the noisy applause given him by the mob because he has spent much on theatres or horse-races for their entertainment is a vain fellow, and is afflicted with the vice to which Aristotle gives the name of vanity; while the man who despises the applause and thinks it little better than the noise of waves beating on the shore, but values more than anything else the approval without flattery which good men bestow on virtue, he is truly great-hearted and high-minded.

[1] Reading in R. 89. 22 διορίζων.

LOGICAL WORKS

TESTIMONIA

ALEX. *in Top.* 5. 17–19. Of this so-called dialectic Aristotle has treated both in other books and particularly in these, which are called *Topics*.

Ibid. 27. 11. Perhaps he would apply the phrase 'mental gymnastic' to a discussion which probes both sides of a question. This type of discussion was not unusual with the ancients. . . . 14–18. They put forward a thesis, and practised on it their[1] inventiveness in argument, establishing and refuting[2] the thesis by probable arguments. There are books both of Aristotle and of Theophrastus containing such arguments from probable premisses to opposite conclusions.

Cf. ELIAS *in Cat.* 133. 9–17.

THEON, *Prog.* 2, p. 165. Examples of training in theses may be got both from Aristotle and from Theophrastus; there are many books of theses bearing their names.

[1] Reading in R. 105. 8 αὐτῶν, with Wallies.
[2] Reading in R. 105. 9 κατασκευάζοντές τε καὶ ἀνασκευάζοντες, with the MSS.

ON PROBLEMS

1 (R^1 109, R^2 112)

ALEX. *in Top.* 62. 30. One might consider in which class of problems one should include such problems as 'Why does the magnetic stone attract iron?', or 'What is the nature of prophetic waters?' These do not seem to fall under any of the recognized kinds. Is it that these are not dialectical problems at all, such as those which we are discussing and whose kinds we are distinguishing? . . . 63. 11–19. Are these not physical problems, as Aristotle has said in his work *On Problems*? Physical phenomena whose causes are unknown constitute physical problems. Still, there are dialectical problems even about physical matters, as there are about ethical and logical matters; those of one kind are dialectical, those of another physical. All dialectical problems will be reducible to the inquiry whether the connexion of an attribute with a thing is a fact, and the inquiry whether a thing exists, which are two of the four questions enumerated at the beginning of the second book of the *Posterior Analytics*;[1] for the questions 'What is the reason of a connexion?' and 'What is the nature of a thing?' are *not* dialectical problems.

[1] Ch. 1.

DIVISIONS

1 (R^2 110, R^3 113)

ALEX. *in Top.* 242. 1–9. 'Moreover, what is itself nobler and more precious and praiseworthy is more desirable than what is less so.' Aristotle here uses the phrases 'nobler', 'more precious', 'more praiseworthy' in a wide sense. In the division of goods he reserves the word 'precious' for the more primary good things, such as gods, ancestors, happiness, the words 'noble' and 'praiseworthy' for the virtues and virtuous activities, the word 'capacities' for those things which may be used well or ill, the word 'useful' for what produces these same goods or contributes towards them. But *here* he seems to apply the words 'noble', 'praiseworthy', and 'precious' even to things that are good as capacities.

2 (R^2 111, R^3 114)

DIOG. LAERT. 3. 80 (45). Plato, according to Aristotle, used to divide things in this way: of goods some are in the soul, some in the body, some external. For example, justice, wisdom, courage, temperance, and the like are in the soul, beauty, good condition, health, and strength in the body; friends, the happiness of one's country, and wealth fall among external goods. . . . 107 (74). Of existing things some exist in their own right, others are relative. . . . 109 (74). It was thus that, according to Aristotle, Plato classified primary things as well.

3 (R^2 112, R^3 115)

COD. MARC. 257, f. 250. Aristotle's *Divisions*. The soul is divided into three elements.

4

SIMP. *in Cat.* 65. 4. In the *Divisions* . . . 7–8 after putting forward the categories he adds: 'I mean these with their cases' (i.e. inflexions).

DISSERTATIONS

I (R^2 113, R^3 116)

Simp. *in Cat.* 64. 18–65. 10. But why, say the followers of Lucius, did he omit the conjunctions, if these too are significant utterances? . . . They also ask where the articles are to be placed. The same account must be given of these. These words also are, as it were, conjunctions which in addition indicate indefinitely the male and the female sexes; for they do not show the essence of anything—which is why some people call them indefinite. But where are negations, privations, and the various inflexions of verbs to be placed? This question Aristotle himself answered in his *Dissertations.* For both in his works on method, in his *Dissertations*, in his *Divisions*, and in another dissertation called *Fallacies depending on Language* (which, even if it is thought by some not to be a genuine work of Aristotle, is at all events the work of some member of the school)—in all of these, after putting forward[1] the categories, he adds, 'I mean these with their cases' (i.e. inflexions), thus connecting the theory of them with that of negations, privations, and indefinite terms.

Dexippus, *in Cat.* 33. 8–13. But where, they say, are negations, privations, and indefinite terms, and the inflexions answering to each category, to be placed? Aristotle himself dealt better with this matter in his *Dissertations*; he put forward the categories, with their 'cases' and with negations and indefinite terms, and thus connected together the theory of all these things; by cases he meant inflexions.

[1] Reading in R. 108. 3 προθείς, with Kalbfleisch.

CATEGORIES

TESTIMONIA

PS.-AMM. *in Cat.* (Ven. 1546), f. 13 *a.* Indeed, they say that in the Great Library there have been found forty books of *Analytics* and two of *Categories*; it was judged by the commentators that of the *Categories* this one was a genuine work of Aristotle. . . . This judgement was based on the thoughts expressed, on the language, and on the fact that the Philosopher has in his other treatises always mentioned this book.

Cf. ELIAS, *in Cat.* 133. 9–17.

1 (R^2 114, R^3 117)

SIMP. *in Cat.* 18. 16–21. Adrastus, in his work on the order of Aristotle's treatises, relates that another book of *Categories* is referred to as being by Aristotle—itself short and concise in its language and differing little from the other *Categories*, but starting with the words 'Of existing things, some are. . . .' He records that both versions had the same number of lines, so that he used the word 'short' with reference to the style, implying that each of the proofs was set out concisely.

AMMON. *in Cat.* 13. 20–25. It should be known that in the old libraries forty books of *Analytics* have been found, but only two of *Categories*. One began[1] 'Of existing things, some are called homonymous, others synonymous'. The other, which we now have lying before us, had this introduction: 'Those things are called homonymous which have only their names in common, their definitions being different.'[2] This version has been preferred as being superior in order and in matter, and as everywhere proclaiming Aristotle as its begetter.

[1] Omitting τὴν . . . φημι in R. 108. 28, with Busse.

[2] This is almost identical with the beginning of the *Categories* which have come down to us.

Cf. Ps.-Ammon. *in Cat.* (Ven. 1546), f. 17 *a*, and Schol. in Arist. *Cat.* 33^b25–33 (Brandis).

Boeth. *in Cat.* I. p. 161 d–162 a (Migne). The book is the work of Aristotle and of no other, since in his whole philosophy he consistently maintains the doctrine of this work, and its brevity and subtlety are not unworthy of Aristotle . . . though there exists another work of Aristotle discussing the same topics, containing much the same comments, while differently expressed. But *this* book has been generally regarded as the authentic one.

ON CONTRARIES

TESTIMONIA

ARIST. *Metaph.* 1003^b33–1004^a2. There must be exactly as many species of being as of unity. To investigate the nature of these is the work of a science that is generically one—I mean, for instance, the discussion of the same, the similar, and the other concepts of this sort; and nearly all contraries may be referred to this origin; let us take them as having been investigated in the *Selection of Contraries*.

Ibid. 1054^a29–32. To the One belong (as we indicated graphically in our distinction of the contraries) the same, the like, and the equal, and to plurality belong the other, the unlike, and the unequal.

ALEX. *in Metaph.* 250. 17–19: see p. 122 *infra*.

SYR. *in Metaph.* 61. 12–17. The same, the like, the equal, the straight, and in general the terms on the better side of the list of cognates, are differentiae and as it were species of the One, as the terms on the worse side belong to the Many. The Philosopher himself treated of the subject separately, making a selection of all contraries and classing some under the One, others under the Many.

Cf. ASC. *in Metaph.* 237. 11–13 (p. 122 *infra*).

SIMP. *in Cat.* 382. 7–10. Aristotle seems to have taken what he says about contraries from the Archytean book entitled *On Contraries*, which he did not group with his discussion of genera, but thought worthy of a separate treatise.

Ibid. 407. 15. Now that Aristotle's account of the difference between opposites has been completed, it would be well to quote Archytas' discussion of them . . . . 19–20. For anyone who had examined Aristotle's book *On Contraries* could not have neglected Archytas' book.

1 (R^2 115, R^3 118)

SIMP. *in Cat.* 387. 17. But now that the language of Aristotle has been clarified, let us see what the more famous interpreters make of the passage. The Stoics pride themselves on their working out of logical problems, and in the matter of contraries, as well as in all other matters, they are anxious to show that Aristotle furnished the starting-point for everything in one book which he called *On Opposites*, in which, too, there is an immense number of problems set forth; of which they have set out a small portion. The others of these it would not be reasonable to include in an introduction, but those which the Stoics set out in agreement with Aristotle must be mentioned. Aristotle laid down an ancient definition of contraries, which we have mentioned previously, viz. that they are the things which differ most from one another within a genus; but in his work on opposites Aristotle subjected this definition to all manner of tests, and amended it. He raised the question whether things that differ[1] are contraries, and whether difference can be contrariety, and whether[2] complete divergence is maximum difference, and whether the things that are farthest apart are identical with those that differ most, and what distance is[3] and how we are to understand maximum distance. These difficulties having been observed, something (he maintained) must be added to the phrase 'the genus', so that the definition comes to be 'the things that are farthest apart in the *same* genus'. He pointed out the difficulties consequent on this; he asked whether contrariety is otherness,[4] and whether the things that are most different are contraries, and added many other criticisms. . . . 388. 13–14. This is but a small part of the difficulties raised by Aristotle in his work on contrarieties.

[1] Omitting the second *καί* in R. 110. 9, with Hayduck.
[2] Reading in R. 110. 10 *δύναται, καὶ εἰ*, with the MSS.
[3] Reading in R. 110. 13 *καὶ τίς ἡ ἀπόστασις*, with the MSS.
[4] Reading in R. 110. 16 *εἰ ἑτερότης ἐστίν*, with Brandis.

2 (R^2 116, R^3 119)

SIMP. *in Cat.* 388. 21. The Stoics used all these distinctions, and in the other distinctions with regard to contraries they followed in Aristotle's steps; he had given them in his treatise on opposites the starting-points which they followed out in their own books. . . . 389. 4–10. Such being the Stoic teaching, let us see how they distorted the Aristotelian tradition. Aristotle in his book on opposites says that justice is contrary to injustice, but that the just man is said not to be contrary, but to be contrariwise disposed, to the unjust man. If even such things as these are contraries, he says, 'contrary' will be used in two senses; it will be applied either with reference to contraries themselves, like virtue and vice, movement and rest, or to things by virtue of a sharing in contraries, e.g. to that which moves and that which rests, or to the good and the bad.

3 (R^2 117, R^3 120)

SIMP. *in Cat.* 389. 25–390. 7. For this reason Chrysippus says that wisdom is contrary to folly, but that the definition of the one is not contrary in the same way to the definition of the other;[1] still, connecting the definitions with the things defined, they oppose the definitions also one to one. This distinction was first drawn by Aristotle, who held that a simple term is not contrary to the definition of its contrary, e.g. that wisdom is not contrary to ignorance of things good, evil, and neutral; but that, if there is contrariety here at all, definition is to be opposed to definition, and that the definitions should be said to be contrary only by being definitions of contrary things. He elaborates further on this, by saying that a definition is contrary to a definition if their subjects are contrary in genus or in differentiae or in both; e.g. let the definition of beauty be 'mutual symmetry of parts'; 'mutual asymmetry of parts' is contrary to this, and the contrariety is in respect of the genus; but in other

[1] i.e. knowledge of things good, things evil, and things neutral, to ignorance of the same.

cases it is by virtue of differentiae; e.g. white is colour that pierces the sight, black is colour that compresses it; in these the genus is the same, but there is contrariety in respect of the differentiae. We have stated, then, how definition is contrary to definition, and[1] how definitions that elucidate essence can be contrary. Let this discussion of the matter suffice.

4 (R² 118, R³ 121)

SIMP. *in Cat.* 390. 19–25. Aristotle himself in his book on opposites considered whether, if someone who has lost one of two things does not of necessity gain the other, there must be a mean between the two, or this is not in all cases so. A man who has lost a true opinion does not necessarily acquire a false one, nor does he who has lost a false opinion necessarily acquire a true one; sometimes he passes from one opinion either to a complete absence of opinion or to knowledge; but there is nothing between true and false opinion except ignorance and knowledge.

5 (R² 119–20, R³ 122–3)

SIMP. *in Cat.* 402. 26. Nicostratus paradoxically takes his start from privations due to custom, and says that privation can always change into positive state. . . . 30. But Aristotle took his distinction between state and privation not from those due to custom but from those that are natural, to which the antithesis of state and privation is primarily applied. Let us use against Nicostratus the very arguments of Aristotle. In his book on opposites he himself says that some privations are privations of natural states, others of customary states, others of possessions, others of other things—blindness a privation of a natural state, nakedness a privation of a customary state, loss of money a privation of something acquired in practice. There are several other types of privation, and some it is impossible, others it is possible, to lose. . . . 403. 5–24. But the full account of privations we can get both from Aristotle's book and from

[1] Reading in R. 111. 29 καὶ οἱ.

that of Chrysippus; Iamblichus has added some remarks which run as follows: '"State" has several meanings, as we have already shown, and "privation" extends to all the meanings of "state", but not to all contraries. For privation is equivalent to loss, so that we cannot talk of privation of evil, since there cannot be a loss of what is evil or harmful, but only of what is good or useful; for a man relieved from disease or poverty would not be said to have been deprived of disease or poverty, though one bereft of health or wealth would be said to have been deprived. Blindness is privation of a good, for sight is a good; nakedness is privation of something indifferent, since raiment is indifferent, neither a good nor an evil. Thus no privation is a good; privation is either an evil or indifferent. There can be privation either of all or of most goods. Aristotle says that of all goods it is those that are in the soul and depend on choice that we can least be deprived of; for no one says he has been deprived of justice, and he who said "No one takes away knowledge" was expressing the same thought. Privations, then, are rather of wealth, reputation, honour, and the like, and most of all of the so-called goods of property; that is why pity and condolence attend on most privations.' But *here*[1] Aristotle has stated the opposition between natural privations and privations of the contraries.[2] So much for this subject.

6 (R^2 121, R^3 124)

SIMP. *in Cat.* 409. 15. Aristotle adds this to what he has said about contraries . . . 17 that the contrary of a good is always an evil, but the contrary of an evil is sometimes a good and sometimes an evil. . . . 30. In the book on opposites he added to these types of contrariety that of things neither good nor evil to things neither good nor evil, saying that white is thus contrary to black, sweet to bitter, high to low in sound, rest to movement. . . . 410. 25–30. Nicostratus urges, as one criticism, that Aristotle's division of contraries is incomplete, since he did not add that indifferent can be opposed

[1] i.e. in the *Categories*.

[2] i.e. of things contrary to the things which natural privations are privations of.

to indifferent. Aristotle added this in the book on opposites, saying that there is a type of opposition between two things neither good nor evil—as we have said before. But he did not call them indifferent, the reason being[1] (I suppose) that the term 'indifferent' was later, being invented by the Stoics.

[1] Reading in R. 114. 9 διότι, with some MS. support.

PHILOSOPHICAL WORKS

ON THE GOOD

TESTIMONIA

ARISTOX. *Harm.* 2. 30. 16–31. 3 (Macran). This, as Aristotle always used to say, was the experience of most of those who heard Plato's lecture *On the Good*. Each of them attended on the assumption that he would gain one of the recognized human goods, such as wealth, health, strength—in general, some marvellous happiness. When Plato's discourses turned out to be about mathematics—numbers, geometry, astronomy—and, to crown all, about the thesis that there is one Good, it seemed to them, I fancy, something quite paradoxical; and so some people despised the whole thing, while others criticized it.

ARIST. *Ph.* 209^{b}11–16. This is why Plato in the *Timaeus* says that matter and space are the same; for the 'participant' and space are identical. It is true, indeed, that the account he gives there of the 'participant' is different from what he says in his so-called 'unwritten doctrines'. Nevertheless, he did identify place and space.

THEM. *in Ph.* 106. 21–23. Yet in the *Timaeus* Plato says that matter receives the Forms in one way, and in the unwritten doctrines says it receives them in another way; in the *Timaeus* he says it is by participation, in the unwritten doctrines by assimilation.

PHILOP. *in Ph.* 521. 9–15. . . . i.e. naming matter differently in the *Timaeus* and in the unwritten doctrines, i.e. in the unwritten lectures; for in the unwritten lectures he called matter great and small (as Aristotle said previously; we have stated why matter is great and small), but in the

Timaeus he calls matter the participant because it participates in the Forms. Aristotle himself copied out Plato's unwritten lectures.

SIMP. *in Ph.* 503. 10–15. Having shown that the infinite is enclosed rather than encloses, and is by its own nature unknowable, Aristotle criticizes the superficial interpretation of Plato's words. Plato in his account of the Good called matter (which he said was indefinite) the great and the small, and said that all sensible things are enclosed by the infinite, and are unknowable because their nature involves matter and is indefinite and in a state of flux.

Ibid. 542. 9–12. Aristotle says that Plato gives matter different names in the *Timaeus* and in the unwritten lectures; in the *Timaeus* he calls it the participant (for it participates 'most obscurely in the intelligible'), but in the unwritten lectures he called it great and small.

Cf. ibid. 545. 23–25, PHILOP. *in Ph.* 515. 29–32.

ARIST. *De An.* 404^b16–21: see p. 83 *supra*.

PHILOP. *in De An.* 75. 34–76. 1. By the books *On Philosophy* Aristotle means the work entitled *On the Good*[1]; in this Aristotle reports Plato's unwritten lectures; the work is genuine. He relates there the view of Plato and the Pythagoreans about realities and first principles.

Cf. SIMP. *in De An.* 28. 7–9, p. 83 *supra*.

ASC. *in Metaph.* 77. 2–4. Yet we say there are no Ideas of evil things; for evil things have no substantial existence but are incidental, as is said in the Platonic lectures.

1 (R^2 22, R^3 27)

Vita Arist. Marciana, p. 433. 10–15 (Rose). Aristotle's character was remarkable for its moderation; he says in the *Categories* that one should not express an opinion hastily,

[1] Philoponus is mistaken; Aristotle means what he says.

but only after repeated consideration, and indeed that even the mere examination of difficulties has its uses; and in the work *On the Good* he says 'not only he who is in luck but also he who offers a proof should remember that he is but a man'.

2 (R^2 23, R^3 28)

Alex. *in Metaph.* 55. 20–57. 28. Both Plato and the Pythagoreans assumed numbers to be the first principles of existing things, because they thought that it is that which is primary and incomposite that is a first principle, and that planes are prior to bodies (for that which is simpler than another and not destroyed with it is prior to it by nature), and on the same principle lines are prior to planes, and points (which the mathematicians call *semeia* but *they* called units) to lines, being completely incomposite and having nothing prior to them; but units are numbers; therefore numbers are the first of existing things. And since Forms or Ideas are prior to the things which according to Plato have their being in relation to them and derive their being from them (the existence of these he tried in several ways to establish), he called the Forms numbers. For if that which is one in kind is prior to the things that exist only in relation to it,[1] and nothing is prior to number, the Forms are numbers. This is the reason why he called the first principles of number first principles of the Forms, and the One the first principle of all things.

Again, the Forms are the first principles of all other things, and since the Ideas are numbers the first principles of number are first principles of the Ideas; and he used to say that the first principles of number are the unit and the dyad. For, since there are in numbers both the One and that which is other than the One (i.e. the many and few), he assumed that the first thing there is in numbers, apart from the One, is the first principle both of the many and of the few. Now the dyad is the first thing apart from the One, having in itself both manyness and fewness; for the double is many and the half is few, and these exist in the dyad; and the dyad

[1] Reading πρὸς αὐτὸ ὄντων.

is contrary to the One, since the latter is indivisible and the former is divided.

Again, thinking that he was proving that the equal and the unequal are first principles of all things, both of things that exist in their own right and of opposites (for he tried to reduce all things to these as their simplest elements), he assigned equality to the monad, and inequality to excess and defect; for inequality involves two things, a great and a small, which are respectively excessive and defective. This is why he called it the indefinite dyad—because neither the excessive nor the defective is, as such, definite; they are indefinite and unlimited. But when limited by the One the indefinite dyad, he says, becomes the numerical dyad; for this kind of dyad is one in form.

Again, the dyad is the first number; its first principles are the excessive and the defective, since it is in the dyad that the double and the half are first found; for while the double and the half are respectively excessive and defective, the excessive and the defective are not necessarily double and half; so that these are elements in the double. And since the excessive and the defective when they have been limited become double and half (for these are no longer unlimited, nor is the threefold and the third part, or the fourfold and the quarter, or anything else that already has its excess limited), and this limitation is effected by the nature of the One (for each thing is one in so far as it is a 'this' and is limited), the One and the great and the small must be elements in the numerical dyad. But the dyad is the first number. These, then, are the elements in the dyad. It is for some such reasons that Plato used to treat the One and the dyad as the first principles both of numbers and of all existing things, as Aristotle says in his work *On the Good*.

Aristotle says here[1] that it is for this reason also that Plato 'made one of his first principles a dyad—because the numbers, with the exception of the first numbers, are neatly produced from it as from a matrix.' This is because he thinks the dyad divides everything to which it is applied; that is why he called it duplicative. For, by making into two each

[1] i.e. in the *Metaphysics*.

of the things to which it is applied, it in a sense divides it, not allowing it to remain what it was; which division is the genesis of numbers. As matrices and moulds make all the things fitted into them to be like, so too the dyad, being as it were a matrix for the successive numbers, becomes generative of them, making two of, or doubling, everything to which it is applied. For when applied to 1 it makes 2 (for twice 1 is 2), when applied to 2 it makes 4 (for twice 2 is 4), when applied to 3 it makes 6 (for twice 3 is 6), and so too in every other case.

By 'except the first numbers' Aristotle means 'except the odd numbers'. For the genesis of odd numbers does not take place in this way—by doubling or by division into two. Here, then, he means by 'first numbers' all the odd numbers without exception; for these are usually treated as prior to even numbers. By 'first numbers' simply is meant numbers divided only by the unit, e.g. 3, 5, and 7 (though 2 also has this characteristic); by 'numbers first relatively to one another' those that have 1 as their only common factor, though they are themselves measurable also by some number. 8 and 9 are so related, for 1 is their only common measure, though each of them has also a number as a factor; 8 has 2 and 4; 9 has 3. Here, however, Aristotle must mean by 'first' all the odd numbers, as being prior to the even; for none of them is generated by the dyad in the aforesaid way; it is by the addition of a unit to each of the even numbers that the odd numbers are produced—a unit which is not the One that acts as first principle (for this was a formative and not a material principle), but as the great and the small when limited by the One became 2, so each of the two when limited by the One is said to be a unit.

Cf. ALEX. apud SIMP. *in Ph.* 454. 19–455. 11.

ALEX. *in Metaph.* 85. 16–18. The first principles are the One and the indefinite dyad, as he has said shortly before and has himself related in the work *On the Good*.

SIMP. *in Ph.* 151. 6–19. Alexander says: 'According to Plato the first principles[1] of all things, and of the Ideas themselves, are the One and the indefinite dyad, which he used to call great and small, as Aristotle relates in his work *On the Good.*' One might gather this also from Speusippus and Xenocrates and the others who were present at Plato's lecture on the Good; for they all wrote down and preserved his doctrine, and they say he used these as first principles. That Plato should call the One and the indefinite dyad first principles of all things is very natural (for the account is a Pythagorean one, and Plato in many respects clearly follows the Pythagoreans); but to call the indefinite dyad, i.e. the great and small, first principles even of the Ideas, indicating by these phrases matter, how can this be consistent, when Plato limits matter to the sensible world and says clearly in the *Timaeus* that it is confined to becoming, and that in it that which comes to be comes to be? Besides, he used to say that the Ideas are known by thought, but that matter is 'credible only to bastard reasoning'.

Ibid. 453. 25–454. 19. They say that Plato maintained that the One and the indefinite dyad were the first principles of sensible things as well. He placed the indefinite dyad also in the objects of intelligence and used to call it 'indeterminate', and he made the great and the small first principles and called them indeterminate, in his lectures on the Good; Aristotle, Heraclides, Hestiaeus, and other associates of Plato attended these and wrote them down in the enigmatic style in which they were delivered. Porphyry, undertaking to put them into articulate shape, has written as follows about them in his *Philebus*: 'The Master assumes the more and the less, and the more and the less intense, to fall under the heading of the indefinite. For where these are present, alternately intensified and relaxed, that which shares in them does not stand still and come to an end, but goes on towards the indefiniteness of infinity. So too with the greater and the smaller, and with Plato's equivalent for them, the great and the small. For let there be a limited magnitude such as a cubit. Let it be bisected and let us leave one half-cubit

[1] Reading in R. 41. 9 ἀρχαί, with Diels.

undivided, but let us cut up the other half-cubit and add it little by little to the undivided part; the cubit will then have two parts, one advancing without end to the less and the other to the greater. For we should never in our cutting come to an indivisible part, since the cubit is a continuum, and a continuum is divided into ever divisible parts. Such an uninterrupted process of cutting shows that there is a certain character of indefiniteness enclosed in the cubit, or rather more than one, the one proceeding towards the great and the other towards the small. In this example the indefinite dyad, also, is seen to be composed of the unit in the direction of the great and that in the direction of the small. And these belong both to continuous bodies and to numbers; for 2 is the first even number, and in the nature of the even are included both the double and the half—the double involving excess, and the half deficiency. So there are excess and deficiency in even number. Now the first even number is 2; it is in itself indefinite, but was limited by sharing in the One; for 2 is limited in so far as it is a single form. Thus the One and the dyad are the elements of numbers as well, the one limiting and giving form, the other indefinite and involving excess and deficiency.' This is almost word for word what Porphyry said, in fulfilment of his promise to explain what was said obscurely in Plato's lecture on the Good; he presumably added that these views were in accordance with what had been written in the *Philebus*.

3 (R² 24, R³ 29)

SEXT. EMP. *Geom.* 57. But Aristotle, at least, says . . . that the length without breadth of which the geometers speak is not unintelligible, but that we can without any difficulty arrive at the thought of it. He rests his argument on a rather clear and indeed a manifest illustration. We grasp the length of a wall, he says, without attending also to its breadth, so that it must be possible to conceive of the length without breadth of which geometers speak.

Cf. SEXT. EMP. *Phys.* I. 412.

4 (R^2 25, R^3 30)

ALEX. APHR. *in Metaph.* 59. 28–60. 2. One might ask how it is that, though Plato mentions both an efficient cause (where he says 'The maker and father of the universe it were a task to find and declare'[1]), and also the final cause (where he says 'Everything exists in relation to the king of all things and for his sake'),[2] Aristotle mentions neither of these causes in his account of Plato's doctrines. Is it because Plato mentioned neither of these in what he said about causes (as Aristotle has shown in his book *On the Good*), or because Plato does not treat these as causes of things that come into being and perish, and did not even work out any theory about them?

5 (R^2 26, R^3 31)

ALEX. *in Metaph.* 250. 17–20. For the proof that practically all contraries are referred to the One and plurality as their first principle, Aristotle sends us to the *Selection of Contraries*, where he has treated expressly of the subject. He has spoken about this selection also in the second book *On the Good*.

Cf. ibid. 262. 18–26.

ASC. *in Metaph.* 237. 11–14. For the information that almost all contraries are reducible to the One and Plurality as to their first principles, Aristotle refers to the *Selection of Contraries*. He has spoken of the selection also in the second book *On the Good*.

Cf. ibid. 247. 17–19.

PS.-ALEX. *in Metaph.* 615. 14–17. Aristotle has made a distinction in his book *On the Good* . . . by which he reduced all contraries to Plurality and the One. To the One belong the same, like, and equal, to Plurality others, unlike, and unequal.

Cf. ibid. 642. 38–643. 3, 695. 23–26.

[1] *Tim.* 28 c. [2] *Ep.* 2. 312 e.

6

ASC. *in Metaph.* 79. 7–10. The Platonists are more, and indeed most, zealous for the existence of the first principles; for in their eyes these are first principles even of the Ideas themselves. They are, as has been said a little earlier, the One and the indefinite dyad; and Aristotle has himself stated this in his book *On the Good*.

ON IDEAS

1 (R² 180, R³ 185)

SYRIAN. *in Metaph.* 120. 33–121. 4. That Aristotle has nothing more than this to say against the theory of Forms is shown both by the first book of this treatise and by the two books he wrote about the Forms; for it is by borrowing practically these same arguments everywhere, and sometimes cutting them up and subdividing them, sometimes proclaiming them more concisely, that he tries to correct his predecessors in philosophy.

Ibid. 195. 10–15. These are the arguments which Aristotle here uses against the theories of the Pythagoreans and the Platonists; which contain also those used in book A major, as the commentator Alexander indicated; for which reason we, having opposed these arguments, do not consider that we have neglected those others—nor yet those which Aristotle has used against those thinkers in his two books on Forms; for there he goes the round of practically these same arguments.

PS.-ALEX. *in Metaph.* 836. 34–837. 3. Aristotle sums up the whole discussion by saying 'The consequences'—for those who assume the existence of the ideal numbers and the separate existence of mathematical entities, and make them causes of physical things—'are those we have stated, and yet more than these might be collected'; he refers to the two books written by him on the Forms—books different from books M and N of the *Metaphysics* and falling outside its plan.

2 (R² 181, R³ 186)

SCHOL. ad DION. THRAC. p. 116. 13–16 (Hilgard). It must be recognized that definitions are of things universal and eternal, as Aristotle has said in the work *On Ideas* which he wrote against Plato's Ideas. Particular things all change and never remain the same; universals are unchangeable and eternal.

3 (R^2 182, R^3 187)

ALEX. APHR. *in Metaph.* 79. 3. The Platonists used the sciences in more than one way to establish the existence of Ideas—as Aristotle relates in the first book of his work *On Ideas*; the arguments he here seems to refer to are as follows: (1) If every science does its work with reference to one self-identical thing, and not to any particular thing, there must be, corresponding to each science, something other than sensible things, which is eternal and is the pattern for the products of the science in question. Now that is just what the Idea is. (2) The things of which there are sciences must exist; now the sciences are concerned with things other than particular things; for the latter are indefinite and indeterminate, while the objects of the sciences are determinate; therefore there are things other than the particulars, and these are the Ideas. (3) If medicine is the science not of this particular instance of health, but just of health, there must be such a thing as health-itself, and if geometry is knowledge not of this equal and this commensurate, but of what is just equal and what is just commensurate, there must be an equal-itself and a commensurate-itself, and these are the Ideas.

Such arguments do not prove the point at issue, that there are Ideas, but they do show that there are things other than sensible particulars. It does not follow, however, that if there are things other than particulars these are Ideas; for besides particulars there are universals, which we maintain to be the objects of the sciences. Take, again, the argument that there must be Ideas of the products of the arts, since every art refers its products to some standard, and the objects of the arts must exist, and must be different from particular things. The latter argument, besides failing, like the others, to prove the existence of Ideas, will be seen to involve Ideas of things of which the Platonists insist that there are no Ideas. For if, because the medical art is knowledge, not of this particular instance of health but simply of health, there is such a thing as health-itself, there will be a similar object of each of the arts. For an art is concerned not with the particular, with the 'this', but simply with that which is the object of the art; e.g. carpentry with bench simply, not with this particular bench, with bed simply, not with this bed; so too are sculpture, painting, building, and each of the other arts, related to their own objects. There will, therefore, be an Idea of each of the objects of the arts—which the believers in the Ideas do not want. . . .

80. 8. They also use the following argument to establish the existence of the Ideas. If each of the many men is a man, and each of the many animals an animal, and so too in all other cases, and these are not instances of a thing being predicated of itself, but there is something predicated of all men, &c., but identical with none of them, there must be something belonging to all of them, which is separate from the particular things and eternal; for in every case it is predicated alike of all the numerically different examples. But that which is one over many, separated from the many and eternal, is an Idea; therefore there are Ideas.

This argument, Aristotle says, involves the Platonists in setting up Ideas even of negations and of non-existent things. For even a negative term is predicated as a single identical term of many subjects, and even of non-existent things, and is not the same as any of these subjects. 'Not-man' is predicated both of horse and of dog and of everything except man, and therefore is a one over many, and identical with none of the things of which it is predicated. Again, it remains always similarly predicable of similar things; for 'not-musical' is predicable truly of many things (of all that are not musical), and similarly 'not-man' of all that are not men; so that there are Ideas even of negations. Which is absurd; for how could there be an Idea of non-existence? If one is to accept such Ideas, there will be one Idea of dissimilar and wholly different objects, e.g. of line and man; for neither of these is a horse. Again, there will be a single Idea of an indefinite variety of objects. Again, there will be a single Idea both of what is primary and of what is secondary; for both man and animal are not-wood, but the one is primary, the other secondary, and of such things the Platonists did not claim that there are genera or Ideas. It is clear that this argument, like the others, does not prove the existence of Ideas; it, like the others, tends to show that that which is predicated in common is different from the particulars of which it is predicated. Again, the very people who wish to show that that which is predicated of many things in common is a single thing, and that this is an Idea, devise a proof from negations. For if one who denies something of several things must do so with reference to a single term—if one who says of a man and of a horse that they are not white does not deny of each of them a separate attribute, but referring to a single thing denies an identical whiteness of both of them—then he who affirms the same term of several things does not affirm something different in each case. There must be some one thing that he affirms; e.g. in predicating 'man' he is referring to one identical thing; for what is true of negation must be true of affirmation. There is, therefore, something apart from what there is in sensible things, something that accounts for affirmation that is true of many things and common to them, and this is the Idea. . . .

81. 25. The argument which establishes the existence of Ideas on the basis of the fact of knowledge is as follows: If when we think of man or land-animal or animal, we think of something real and at the same time not a particular (for the same thought remains even when the particular things have perished), clearly there is something apart from sensible particulars, something which we apprehend both when they exist and when they do not; for surely we do not then apprehend something non-existent. This is a Form or Idea. . . .

82. 11. The argument that establishes Ideas answering even to relative terms is as follows: When the same term is predicated of several things not homonymously but so as to indicate a single nature, it is predicable truly of them either because they have in the strict sense the property indicated by the predicate (as when we say Socrates is a man and Plato is a man), or because they are likenesses of the true

possessors of the attribute (as when we predicate 'man' of men in pictures (for in these cases we refer to the likenesses of men, indicating a nature that is identical in them all)), or because one of them is the pattern and the others are likenesses (as when we call both Socrates and the likenesses of him 'men'). We predicate of things in this world equality itself, which is only homonymously predicable of them; for neither does the same definition apply to them all, nor are we referring to things truly equal. For a sensible thing's size changes and varies continuously and is not determinate, nor does anything in this world answer precisely to the definition of equality. Nor, again, are they related as pattern and image; for one is not more pattern or image than another. Even if one were to allow that an image is not merely homonymous with its pattern, it always follows that particular equal things are equal only as being images of that which is strictly and truly equal. If this be so, there is an equal itself, a strictly equal, by reference to which things in this world, as being images of it, come to be, and are said to be, equal, and this is an Idea, serving as a pattern to the things[1] that come into being by reference to it. . . .

83. 22–30. This is the argument which according to Aristotle implies Ideas answering even to relative terms. At all events the proof in question has referred to equality, which is a relative term; but the Platonists denied that there are Ideas answering to relative terms, because for them Ideas exist in their own right, being substances, while relative terms have their being in their relation to one another. Again, if what is equal is equal to what is equal to it, there will be more than one Idea of the equal; for the equal-itself is equal to the equal-itself, since if it were not equal to anything it would not even be equal. Again, according to the same argument there will have to be ideas even of unequals (for where there are opposites there must be Ideas either of both or of neither); but even the Platonists admit that inequality involves more than one thing.

[1] Reading *παραδειγματικὸν ὂν τοῖς κτλ.*

4 (R^2 183, R^3 188)

ALEX. APHR. *in Metaph.* 83. 34. The argument which introduces the third man was as follows: The Platonists say that the things that are predicated universally of substances are precisely such as they are said to be, and that these are Ideas.[1] They say, too, that things that are like one another are so by sharing in one identical thing, which is strictly what it is; and that this is the Idea. But if this be so, and if that which is predicated of certain things in common must, if it is not identical with any of them, be something else apart from them (for that is why man-himself is a genus—because while predicated of particular men it was identical with none of them), there will be a third man apart from the particular man (e.g. Socrates or Plato), and apart from the Idea, which is itself also numerically one. . . .

84. 21. The existence of the third man is also proved in this way. If that which is predicated truly of several things also exists in se[illegible]n from these (this is what the believers in Ideas think they prove; the reason why, according to them, man-himself exists is that 'man' is predicated truly of the many particular men, and is other than they)—if this be so, there will be a third man. For if the 'man' which is predicated is different from those of whom it is predicated, and exists independently, and 'man' is predicated both of particular men and of the Idea of man, there will be a third man apart both from particular men and from the Idea. On this basis, too, there will be a fourth man, predicated both of the third man, of the Idea, and of the particulars; and similarly a fifth, and so *ad infinitum*. This argument is identical with the first, and follows from the assumptions that things that are like are like by participation in some identical thing, and that particular men and the Ideas are like. . . . 85. 9. The first exposition of the 'third man' has been used by others and plainly by Eudemus in his book *On Diction*, and Aristotle himself has used the last in the fourth book of his work *On Ideas*, and also, a little later, in the *Metaphysics*. . . .

[1] Reading in R. 150. 27–28 εἶναι ἰδέας, with Asclepius.

85. 18. Aristotle says that these arguments, used to establish the existence of Ideas, destroy these first principles; and with these will be destroyed the things that come after the first principles, if indeed they proceed from the first principles; so that the Ideas also will be destroyed. For if in the case of all things that have a common predicate there is something separate, the Idea, and if twoness is predicated even of the indefinite dyad, there will be something—an Idea—prior to the indefinite dyad, which will then no longer be a first principle. But neither will duality, in its turn, be primary, a first principle; for of it again, as being an Idea, number is predicable; for the Ideas are assumed by the Platonists to be numbers; so that for them number will be the first thing, being an Idea. But if this be so, number will be prior to the indefinite dyad (which is for them a first principle), not the dyad to number; and if so, the dyad will no longer be a first principle, if it is what it is by sharing in something. Again, the dyad is assumed to be a first principle of number, but according to the argument just stated number becomes prior to it; but if number is relative (for every number is the number of something), and if number is the first of existing things (since it is prior even to the dyad, which they assumed to be a first principle), that which is relative will be according to them prior to that which exists in its own right. But this is absurd; for everything that is relative is secondary. For a relative term indicates the possession of a pre-existent nature which is prior to the possession that occurs to it. . . . 86. 11. But even if one were to say that number is a quantity and not a relation, it would follow for the Platonists that quantity is prior to substance; but the great and the small themselves are relative. Again, it follows that they must say that that which is relative is a first principle of and prior to that which exists in its own right, inasmuch as for them the Idea is the first principle of substances, and the Idea's being an Idea depends on its being a pattern, and a pattern is relative, being the pattern for something. Again, if the being of Ideas depends on their being patterns, the things which come into being in relation to them, and which the Ideas are Ideas of, must be

copies of them, and so one might say that according to these thinkers all natural objects turned out to be relative; for all are either images or patterns. Again, if the being of the Ideas depends on their being patterns, and a pattern exists for the sake of that which comes into being in relation to it, and that which exists for the sake of something else is inferior to it, the Ideas will be inferior to the things that come into being in relation to them. . . .

87. 3. Such are the arguments which, in addition to those previously mentioned, by means of the theory of Ideas undermine the foundations of the theory. If that which is predicated of certain things in common is the first principle and Idea of them, and if 'first principle' is predicated of all first principles in common, and 'element' of all elements, there will be something that is prior to, and a first principle of, first principles and elements; and so there will be neither a first principle nor an element. Again, Idea is not prior to Idea; for all Ideas are alike first principles. But the One-itself and the Two-itself, Man-himself, Horse-itself, and each of the other Ideas is for these thinkers alike an Idea; therefore none of them will be prior to another, and therefore none will be a first principle; therefore the One and the indefinite dyad are not first principles. Again, it is paradoxical that an Idea should derive its form from an Idea, for all Ideas are forms; but if the One and the indefinite dyad are first principles, one Idea will derive its form from another—the dyad itself from the One itself; for that is how they are said to be first principles—the One as form, the dyad as matter; therefore these are not first principles. But if they say that the indefinite dyad is not an Idea, then in the first place, though it is a first principle there will be something prior to it—the dyad itself, by participation in which the indefinite dyad is itself a dyad; for the indefinite dyad is not the dyad itself, since it is only by virtue of participation that 'dyad' will be predicated of it, as of particular pairs of things. Again, if the Ideas are simple, they cannot be derived from two different first principles, but the One and the indefinite dyad are different. Again, the number of the dyads will be surprising, if there is first the dyad-itself, then the indefinite

dyad, then the mathematical dyad we use in counting (which is not identical with either of the other two), and then in addition that which exists in numerable and sensible things. These consequences are paradoxical, so that clearly by following out the assumptions made by these thinkers about the Ideas it is possible to destroy the first principles, which are for them more important than the Ideas. . . .

88. 20–89. 7. Again, the argument which says that the cause of things happening in an orderly way is their being made after a fixed pattern, which is the Idea, applies not only to substances. There is also the argument which starts from what we assert truly, and maintains that this must exist. Now in saying that there are five (or three) forms of harmony, and three concordant intervals, we assert truly; therefore there are just so many; but the number of such things in the sensible world is infinite; therefore there are other, eternal, objects with reference to which what we say is true. Thus this argument, also, applies not only to substances. And there are many other such arguments.

5 (R² 184, R³ 189)

ALEX. APHR. *in Metaph.* 97. 27–98. 24. To prove that it is not, as Eudoxus and some others thought, by the intermixture of Ideas that other things exist, Aristotle says it is easy to collect many impossible conclusions that follow from this opinion. These would be as follows: If the Ideas are mixed with other things, (1) they will be bodies; for it is to bodies that mixture appertains. (2) Ideas will be contrary to one another; for it is between contraries that mixture occurs. (3) Mixture will take place in such a way that either an Idea will be present whole in each of the things with which it is mixed, or only a part of it will be present. But if it is present whole, something that is numerically one will be present in several things (for the Idea is numerically one); but if mixture be by way of parts, it will be that which shares in a part of man-himself, not that which shares in the whole of man-himself,[1] that will be a man. (4) The Ideas would then be divisible and partible, though they are not subject to change. (5) The Forms must consist of like parts, if all the things that contain a part of a certain Form are like one another. But how can the Forms consist of like parts? A piece of a man cannot be a man, as a piece of gold is gold. (6) As Aristotle himself says a little later, in each thing there will be an admixture not of one Idea but of many; for if there is one Idea of animal and another of man, and a man is both an animal and a man, he will partake of both Ideas. And the Idea man-himself, inasmuch as it is also animal, will share in animal-itself; but on that showing the Ideas will no longer be simple, but composed of many components, and some Ideas will be primary and others secondary. If on the other hand man-himself is not animal—it is surely absurd to say that a man is not an animal.[2] (7) If the Forms are mingled with the things that exist by reference to them, how can they still be patterns, as these thinkers maintain? It is not thus, by mixture, that patterns cause the likeness of the copies of them to them. (8) On this showing, the Ideas would be destroyed along with the things in which they are. Nor would they have a separate existence, but only existence in the things which share in them. (9) On this showing, the Ideas will no longer be exempt from change; and there are all the other absurd implications which Aristotle in the second book of his work *On Ideas* showed this theory to involve. This is why he said 'It would be easy to collect many insuperable objections to this view'; they have been collected in that work.

[1] Reading in R. 152. 7 *οὐ τὸ ὅλον τοῦ αὐτοανθρώπου*, with some MSS. and Hayduck.

[2] sc. 'Yet this follows from saying that man-himself is not animal'.

ON THE PYTHAGOREANS

1[1] (R[2] 186, R[3] 191)

APOLLON. *Mirab.* 6. These were succeeded by Pythagoras son of Mnesarchus, who first worked at mathematics and arithmetic, but later even indulged in miracle-mongering like that of Pherecydes. When a ship was coming into harbour at Metapontum laden with a cargo, and the bystanders were, on account of the cargo, praying for her safe arrival, Pythagoras intervened and said: 'Very well, you will see the ship bearing a dead body.' Again in Caulonia, according to Aristotle, he prophesied the advent of a she-bear; and Aristotle also,[2] in addition to much other information about him, says that in Tuscany he killed a deadly biting serpent by biting it himself. He also says that Pythagoras foretold to the Pythagoreans the coming political strife; by reason of which he departed to Metapontum unobserved by anyone, and while he was crossing the river Cosas he, with others, heard the river say, with a voice beyond human strength, 'Pythagoras, hail!'; at which those present were greatly alarmed. He once appeared both at Croton and at Metapontum on the same day and at the same hour. Once, while sitting in the theatre, he rose (according to Aristotle) and showed to those sitting there that one of his thighs was of gold.[3] There are other surprising things told about him, but, not wishing to play the part of mere transcribers, we will bring our account of him to an end.

AELIAN, *V.H.* 2. 26. Aristotle says that Pythagoras was called by the people of Croton the Hyperborean Apollo. The son of Nicomachus[4] adds that Pythagoras was once seen by many people, on the same day and at the same hour, both

[1] Rose's fr. 190 is omitted because in the text of Clement *Ἀριστοτέλης* is only an emendation of *Ἀρίσταρχος*.

[2] Inserting after *Ἀριστοτέλης* in R. 153. 13 *προυσήμηνε τὴν λευκὴν ἄρκτον* (from Iamb. *V.P.* 142) *καὶ ὁ αὐτὸς Ἀριστοτέλης*, with Diels.

[3] Reading in R. 154. 1 *τοῖς καθημένοις ὡς χρυσοῦν*, with Diels.

[4] i.e. Aristotle.

at Metapontum and at Croton; and at Olympia, during the games, he got up in the theatre and showed that one of his thighs was golden. The same writer says that while crossing the Cosas he was hailed by the river, and that many people heard him so hailed.

Ibid. 4. 17. Pythagoras used to tell people that he was born of more than mortal seed; for on the same day and at the same hour he was seen (they say)[1] at Metapontum and at Croton; and at Olympia he showed that one of his thighs was golden. He informed Myllias of Croton that he was Midas the Phrygian, the son of Gordius. He fondled the white eagle, which made no resistance. While crossing the river Cosas he was addressed by the river, which said 'Hail, Pythagoras!'

DIOG. LAERT. 8. 1. 11 (9). He is said to have been very dignified in his bearing, and his disciples held that he was Apollo, and came from the men of the north. There is a story that once, when he was stripped, his thigh was seen to be golden; and there were many who said that the river Nessus had hailed him as he was crossing it.

IAMB. *V.P.* 28. 140–3. The Pythagoreans derive their confidence in their views from the fact that the first to express them[2] was no ordinary man, but God.[3] One of their traditions relates to the question 'Who art thou, Pythagoras?'[4]; they say he is the Hyperborean Apollo. This is supposed to be evidenced by two facts: when he got up during the games he showed a thigh of gold, and when he entertained Abaris the Hyperborean he stole from him the arrow by which he was guided. Abaris is said to have come from the Hyperboreans collecting money for the temple and prophesying pestilence; he lived in the sacred shrines and was never seen to drink or eat anything; it is said, too, that in Lacedaemon

[1] Reading in R. 154. 17 *φασί*, suggested by Rose.
[2] Reading in R. 155. 3 *αὐτά*, with Kiessling.
[3] Reading in R. 155. 4 *ἀλλ' ὁ θεός*, with the MSS.
[4] Reading in R. 155. 5 *τίς εἶ, Πυθαγόρα;* with Deubner.

he offered preventive sacrifices, and that for this reason there was never again a plague in Lacedaemon. From this Abaris Pythagoras took the golden arrow without which he could not find his way, and so made Abaris witness to his power. At Metapontum, when certain people prayed that they might receive the cargo of the ship that was sailing thither, he said, 'Then you will have[1] a dead man'; and the ship was found to carry a corpse. At Sybaris he seized and dispatched the serpent that had killed the hare, and similarly the little serpent in Tyrrhenia which killed by biting.[2] At Croton (they say) he caressed the white eagle, which made no resistance. When someone wanted to hear him speak, he said he would never speak until a sign had appeared; and after that the white bear appeared in Caulonia. In speech with someone who was about to announce to him the death of his son,[3] he announced it first himself. He told Myllias of Croton that he was Midas the son of Gordius; and Myllias went off to the mainland to do over Midas' tomb what Pythagoras had bidden. They say, too, that the man who bought his house and destroyed it dared tell no one what he had seen, and for this crime was convicted at Croton of sacrilege and put to death; he was found guilty of seizing the golden beard which fell from Pythagoras' statue. These things and others like them are what the Pythagoreans say in confirmation of their belief.

Cf. PORPH. *V.P.* 23–28.

2 (R² 187, R³ 192)

IAMB. *V.P.* 6. 30. Besides, they numbered Pythagoras among the gods, as a good spirit and a great friend to men; some of them identified him with the Pythian, some with the Hyperborean, some with the Paean Apollo, and others with one of the spirits that inhabit the moon. . . . 31. Aristotle relates in his work on the Pythagorean philosophy that the following

[1] Reading in R. 155. 17 ἔσται.
[2] Reading in R. 155. 21 ὄφιν ὃς ἀπέκτεινε, with the MSS.
[3] Reading in R. 156. 2 αὐτῷ τὸν τοῦ υἱοῦ θάνατον, with Cobet.

division was preserved by the Pythagoreans as one of their greatest secrets—that there are three kinds of rational living creatures—gods, men, and beings like Pythagoras.

3 (R^2 188, R^3 193)

APUL. *De Deo Soc.* 20. 166–7. I believe that most of you are reluctant to believe what I have just said, and marvel greatly at Socrates' having had a vision of a divine being. But I suppose Aristotle is a sufficient witness to the fact that the Pythagoreans marvelled at any town-bred person who said he had *never* seen a divine being. Now if anyone can have the power of seeing a divine apparition, why should not such a power have fallen to the lot of Socrates, above all others?

CLEM. AL. *Strom.* 6. 6. 53. 2–3. Isidorus the son and pupil of Basilides, in the first book of his commentary on the prophet Parchor, says himself in so many words: 'The Athenians say certain things were disclosed to Socrates by a divine being which accompanied him; and Aristotle says all men have divine beings which accompany them at the time of their incarnation;' this prophetic teaching he received and set down in his books, without confessing whence he had stolen this account.

4 (R^2 189, R^3 194)

GELL. 4. 11. 11–13. Plutarch also, a scholar of great authority, says in the first of his books on Homer that the philosopher Aristotle had in his writings made the same statement about the Pythagoreans, that they did not abstain from eating animals, except for a few kinds of flesh. Since the fact is not generally recognized, I add Plutarch's own words: 'Aristotle says the Pythagoreans abstain from eating womb and heart, the sea anemone, and certain other such things, but use all other kinds. The sea anemone is a marine animal which is called the nettle.'

PORPH. *V.P.* 45. Pythagoras advised his followers to abstain from other things as well, such as womb, the red mullet, the sea anemone, and indeed almost all other sea creatures.

DIOG. LAERT. 8. 1. 19 (18). Above all, he forbade them to eat erythinus and black-tail; they must also abstain from eating heart or beans; and Aristotle says that at times they must abstain from eating womb or red mullet.

5 (R² 190, R³ 195)

DIOG. LAERT. 8. 1. 33 (19). The Pythagoreans say we should not pay equal honour to gods and to heroes, but to the gods at all times, keeping a guard on our lips, in white raiment and with pure bodies, and to the heroes only from midday onwards. The purity is to be achieved by cleansing rites, by baths, by lustral water, by having no stain from funeral rites, from childbirth,[1] or from any infection, and by abstention from meat that has been nibbled at or has died by disease, and from red mullets, black-tails, eggs and oviparous animals, beans, and the other things that are forbidden to those who perform the sacred rites in temples. Aristotle says, in his work *On the Pythagoreans*,[2] that Pythagoras enjoined abstention from beans either because they are like the privy parts, or because they are like the gates of Hades (for this is the only plant that has no joints), or because they are destructive, or because they are like the nature of the universe, or because they are oligarchical (being used in the choice of rulers by lot). Things that fall from the table they were told not to pick up—to accustom them to eating with moderation, or because such things marked the death of someone. . . . They must not touch a white cock, because this animal is sacred to Lunus and is a suppliant, and supplication is a good thing. The cock was sacred to Lunus because it announces the hours; also, white is of the nature of the good, black of the nature of the bad.[3] They were not to touch

[1] Reading in R. 158. 8 after *κήδους* the words *καὶ λέχους*, omitted by Rose.

[2] Reading in R. 158. 13 after *Ἀριστοτέλης* the words *ἐν τῷ περὶ τῶν Πυθαγορείων*, with some MSS. and Diels.

[3] Reading in R. 158. 21–24 *καὶ τὸ μὲν λευκόν . . . κακοῦ* before *τῶν ἰχθύων . . . δούλοις*, with Diels.

any fish that was sacred, since it was not right that the same dishes should be served to gods and to men, any more than they should to freemen and to slaves. They must not break the loaf (because in old times friends met over a single loaf, as barbarians do to this day), nor must they divide the loaf which brings them together. Others explain the rule by reference to the judgement in Hades; others say that dividing the loaf would produce cowardice in war; others explain that it is from the loaf that the universe starts. . . . 36. These things Alexander says he found in the Pythagorean commentaries; Aristotle records the practices akin to these.

6 (R² 191, R³ 196)

PORPH. *V.P.* 41. Pythagoras said certain things in a mystical and symbolic way, and Aristotle has recorded most of these; e.g. that he called the sea the tear of Cronos, the Bears[1] the hands of Rhea, the Pleiades the lyre of the Muses, the planets the dogs of Persephone; the ringing sound of bronze when struck was, he said, the voice of a divine being imprisoned in the bronze.

AELIAN, *V.H.* 4.17. The origin of earthquakes was, Pythagoras said, nothing but a concourse of the dead; the rainbow was the gleam of the sun, and the echo that often strikes on our ears was the voice of mightier beings.

7 (R² 192, R³ 197)

PORPH. *V.P.* 42. There was also another kind of symbol, illustrated by what follows: 'Step not over a balance', i.e. be not covetous: 'Poke not the fire with a sword', i.e. do not vex with sharp words a man swollen with anger; 'Pluck not the crown', i.e. offend not against the laws, which are the crowns of cities. Or again, 'Eat not heart', i.e. vex not yourself with grief: 'Sit not on the corn ration', i.e. live not in idleness; 'When on a journey, turn not back', i.e. when you are dying, cling not to this life; 'Walk not the highway',

[1] Ursa Major and Minor.

i.e. follow not the opinions of the many but pursue those of the few and educated; 'Receive not swallows in your house', i.e. do not make housemates of talkative men of uncontrolled tongue; 'Add to the burdens of the burdened, lighten them not', i.e. contribute to no man's sloth, to every man's excellence; 'Carry not images of the gods in your rings', i.e. make not your thought and speech about the gods manifest and obvious, nor lay it open to many; 'Make your libations to the gods at the handle of the cup', i.e. honour and celebrate the gods with music; for this rings through the handle.

JEROME, *Adv. Libros Rufini* 3. 39. To the Pythagoreans also belong such sayings as 'Friends have everything in common' . . . and those riddles which Aristotle recounts with care in his books: 'Leap not over a balance', i.e. go not beyond what is just; 'Poke not fire with a sword', i.e. vex not with abusive words a mind swollen with anger; 'Never pluck a crown', i.e. preserve the laws of your cities; 'Eat not heart', i.e. cast sadness from your mind; 'When you have started out, return not', i.e. desire not life itself after death; 'Walk not on the highway', i.e. follow not the errors of the multitude; 'Take no swallow into your house', i.e. have not as housemates garrulous and talkative men; 'Place more burdens on the burdened, help not those who lay burdens down',[1] i.e. encourage those who press on to virtue, abandon those who give themselves to ease.

8 (R² 193, R³ 198)

MART. CAP. 7. 131 (Philosophy speaks). 'Although Aristotle, one of my followers, reasoning from the fact that the unit itself is one alone and wishes to be always sought after, asserts that it is called Desire because it desires itself, since it has nothing beyond itself and, never carried beyond itself or linked with other things, turns its own ardours on itself.'

9 (R² 194, R³ 199)

THEO. SM. *Math*, p. 21. 20 (Hiller). The first division of numbers they recognize is into two kinds, even and odd. . . . 24. Some

[1] Reading in R. 160. 25 *superponendum onus, deponentibus.*

said I was the first odd number. . . . 22. 5–9. But Aristotle in his work *On the Pythagoreans* says that the One partakes of the nature of both kinds; for added to an even number it makes an odd, and added to an odd an even, which it could not have done if it had not shared in both natures; and that for this reason the One was called even-odd.

10 (R^2 195, R^3 200)

SIMP. *in De Cael.* 386. 9. The Pythagoreans reduced all antitheses to two lists of opposites, the one worse, the other better—the list of goods and the list of evils. They rounded off each list symbolically by the decad, as being the complete number, and they took each of the ten antitheses as revealing all its congeners within itself. Of the local positions they took the right and the left . . . 19–23 and explained the other local opposites in the light of these. Right, above, and before they called good, and left, below, and behind evil, as Aristotle himself related in his collection of Pythagorean tenets.

11 (R^2 196, R^3 201)

STOB. I. 18. I[c] (Wachsmuth and Hense). In the first book of his work on the philosophy of Pythagoras Aristotle writes that the heaven was one, and that time and breath and the void, which divides for ever the regions of different things, were drawn in from the infinite.

12 (R^2 197, R^3 202)

ALEX. APHR. *in Metaph.* 75. 15–17. Of the arrangement in the heavens which the Pythagoreans assigned to the numbers, Aristotle informs us in the second book of his work on the doctrine of the Pythagoreans.

13 (R^2 198, R^3 203)

ALEX. APHR. *in Metaph.* 38. 8. Aristotle has shown what are the likenesses that the Pythagoreans believed in between numbers and the things that exist and come into being; assuming that reciprocity or equality is a property of justice and finding it to exist in numbers, they said, for this reason, that justice is the first square number; for in every case the first of a number of things that admit of the same definition is most truly that which it is said to be. Now this number some declared to be the number 4, because, being the first square number, it is divided into equals and is itself equal (being twice 2), while others declared it to be the number 9, which is the first square number produced by multiplying an odd number (3) by itself. Again, they said the number 7 was opportunity; for natural things seem to have their perfect seasons of birth and completion in terms of sevens, as in the case of man. Men are born after seven months, they begin to grow their teeth in seven months, they reach puberty about the end of the second set of seven years, and grow beards about the end of the third. The sun, too, since it is itself thought to be (as he says) the cause of seasons, they maintain to be established where resides the number 7, which they identify with season; for the sun holds the seventh place among the ten bodies that move round the earth or hearth of the universe; it moves after the sphere of the unwandering stars and the five spheres of the planets; after it come the moon, eighth, and the earth, ninth, and after the earth the counter-earth. Since the number 7 neither generates nor is generated by any of the numbers in the decad, they identified it with Athene. For the number 2 generates 4, 3 generates 9, and 6, 4 generates 8, and 5 generates 10, and 4, 6, 8, 9, and 10 are also themselves generated, but 7 neither generates any number nor is generated from any; and so too Athene was motherless and ever-virgin. Marriage, they said, was the number 5, because it is the union of male and female, and according to them the odd is male and the even female, and 5 is the first number generated from the first even number, 2, and the first odd number, 3; for the odd is for them (as I said) male, and the even female. Reason (which was the name they gave to soul) and substance they identified with the One. Because it was unchanging, alike everywhere, and a ruling principle they called reason a unit, or one; but they also applied these names to substance, because it is primary. Opinion they identified with the number 2 because it can move in two directions; they also called it movement and epithesis.[1] Picking out such likenesses between things and numbers, they assumed numbers to be the first principles of things, saying that all things are composed of numbers.

But they also saw the concordant intervals to be constituted according to particular numbers, and said that numbers were the first principles of these also; the octave depends on the ratio 2 : 1, the fifth on the ratio 3 : 2, the fourth on the ratio 4 : 3. They said, too, that the whole universe is constructed in accordance with a certain harmony . . . 39. 24–41. 15 because it consists of numbers and is constructed in accordance with number and harmony. For the bodies that move round the centre of the universe have their distances in a certain ratio, and some move faster and others slower, and in their movement the slower strike a deep note and the faster a high one, and these notes, being proportionate to the distances, make the resultant sound harmonious; and since they said number was the origin of this harmony, they naturally made number the first principle of the heavens and of the universe. For they thought the sun to be, say, twice as far from the earth as the moon, Venus to be three times as far, Mercury four times, and each of the other heavenly bodies to be in a certain ratio, and the movement of the heavens to be harmonious, and the bodies that move the greatest distance to move the fastest, those that move the least distance the slowest, and the intermediate bodies to move in proportion to the greatness of their circuit. On the basis of these likenesses between things and numbers, they supposed existing things both to be composed of numbers and to be numbers.

Thinking numbers to be prior to nature as a whole and to natural things (for nothing could either exist or be known at all without number, while numbers could be known even apart from other things), they laid it down that the elements and first principles of numbers are the first principles of all things. These principles were, as has been said, the even and the odd, of which they thought the odd to be limited and

[1] sc. the addition of 1 to 1.

the even unlimited; of numbers they thought the unit was the first principle, composed of the even and the odd; for the unit was at the same time even-odd, which he[1] used to prove from its power of generating both odd and even number; added to an even it generates an odd, added to an odd it generates an even.

As regards the agreements which they found between numbers and concordant combinations on the one hand, and on the other hand the attributes and parts of the heavens, they took these for granted straight off, as being obvious, and inferred that the heavens are composed of numbers and display a concord. If any of the heavenly phenomena seemed to fail to conform with numerical principles, they made the necessary additions themselves and tried to fill the gap so as to make their whole treatment of the matter self-consistent. Treating the decad straight off as the perfect number, and seeing that in the visible world the moving spheres are nine in number—seven spheres of the planets, the eighth that of the unwandering stars, the ninth the earth (for this, too, they thought, moves in a circle about the resting hearth of the universe, which according to them is fire)—they added, in their system, a counter-earth, which they supposed to move in a direction opposite to that of the earth's movement, and to be for that reason invisible to those on earth.

Aristotle speaks of these matters both in the *De Caelo*[2] and, with greater precision, in his collection of Pythagorean doctrines. They made out the arrangement of those bodies to be harmonious by assuming that the ten moving bodies of which the universe consists are at harmonic distances from each other, and move in proportion to their distances (as Aristotle has said before), some faster, others slower, and that, as they move, the slower moving sound deeper notes and the faster moving higher notes, and that by the harmonious proportions between these a harmonious note is produced, which, however, we do not hear because we have grown up with it from childhood. He has spoken of this also in the *De Caelo*, and shown there that it is not true. That the even is for them the indefinite and the odd the definite, and that these are

[1] Pythagoras. [2] Omitting μέν in R. 162. 19, with Hayduck.

the generating principles of the unit (for it is by derivation from them that it is even-odd), and indeed of all number (since the units in turn are the generating principles of the numbers), and that the whole heavens, i.e. everything that is in the heavens, in other words all existing things, are number—this he says here, but he has spoken of the subject more fully in those other places.

14 (R² 199, R³ 204)

SIMP. *in De Caelo* 511. 25. The Pythagoreans oppose this view; for this is what 'contrariwise' means; they do not say that the earth is at the centre, but that in the centre of the universe there is fire, and that about the centre the counter-earth moves, being itself an earth but called a counter-earth because it is on the opposite side to our earth. 'After the counter-earth came our earth, itself also moving round the centre, and after the earth the moon;' so Aristotle relates in his work on the Pythagorean doctrines.[1] . . . 512. 12–14. For this reason some call fire the tower of Zeus, as Aristotle himself related in his work on the Pythagoreans, while others call it the stronghold of Zeus (so Aristotle says here), or the throne of Zeus (as other authors relate).

Cf. PROCL. *in Eucl.* p. 90. 14 (Friedlein). The Pythagoreans thought fit to call the pole the seal of Rhea . . . 17–18 and the centre of the universe the stronghold of Zeus.

Cf. PROCL. *in Tim.* p. 61 c, SIMP. *in Phys.* 1355. 8–9.

15 (R² 200, R³ 205)

SIMP. *in De Caelo*, 392. 16–32. Aristotle says that the Pythagoreans place us in the upper part and on the right side of the universe, and those opposite to us in the lower part and on the left side; how can he say this if, as he himself relates in the second book of his collection of Pythagorean tenets, they say that one part of the whole universe is up and the other down, the lower part right and the upper left, and that

[1] Reading in R. 163. 1 ἐν τῷ περὶ τῶν Πυθαγορικῶν, with Karsten.

we are in the lower part? Is it that he has used the words 'upper' and 'on the right' here not in accordance with his own view but with that of the Pythagoreans? They coupled 'up' and 'before' with 'right', 'down' and 'behind' with 'left'. But Alexander thinks that the statement in Aristotle's collection of Pythagorean tenets has been altered by someone and should be that the upper part of the universe is on the right, the lower part on the left, and that we are in the upper part, not in the lower as the text now runs; in this way Aristotle's original statement would agree with what he says here, that we, who say we live in the lower part and therefore on the left side (since the lower part is coupled with the left side), are in opposition to the Pythagorean statement that we live in the upper part and on the right side. The suggested corruption of the text is very probable, since Aristotle knows that the Pythagoreans coupled the higher position with the right side, and the lower with the left.

THEM. *in De Caelo*, 96. 17–22. If, indeed, the Pythagoreans say the upper part is that which is on the right side—as appears from Aristotle's criticism of them in his book against the Pythagorean tenets, where he opposes those who contended that the higher region is on the right.

16

STOB. I. 26. 3. Some of the Pythagoreans, according to Aristotle's account and the statement of Philippus of Opus, say that the eclipse of the moon is due to the interposition, sometimes of the earth, sometimes of the counter-earth. Of the younger members of the school there are some who thought it was due to distribution of the flame, which kindles gradually and regularly until it gives the complete light of full moon, and again diminishes correspondingly until the time of conjunction, when it is completely extinguished.

ON THE PHILOSOPHY OF ARCHYTAS

1 (R³ 206)

SIMP. *in De Caelo*, 296. 16–18. These things, then, Aristotle knows. For this reason, in his epitome of Plato's *Timaeus* he writes: 'He says the universe is a generated universe; for he supposes that it is perceptible to sense, and that what is perceptible has been generated, and what is intelligible has not been generated.'

2 (R² 201, R³ 207)

DAMASC. *Pr.* 2. 172. 16–22 (Ruelle). It is better, therefore, to stick to his distinction, treating as 'other', in accordance with the Pythagorean custom and that of Plato himself, things that have matter in their being, and matter itself; for this is how Plato uses the word 'other' in the *Phaedo*,[1] saying that sensible forms are 'other and in things that are other'. Aristotle in his work on Archytas relates that Pythagoras, too, called matter 'other', as being in flux and always becoming different. So it is clear that Plato, too, defines in this way the things that are 'other'.

[1] 83 b.

ON DEMOCRITUS

I (R^2 202, R^3 208)

Simp. *in De Caelo*, 294. 23–295. 26. Alexander adds that those who say the universe is now in this state, now in that, are ascribing to it change of quality, not generation and destruction. 'Those who say the universe is generated and perishable like any other composite thing, must be' (he says) 'the followers of Democritus. For as each other thing, according to them, comes into being and perishes, so does each of the numberless universes. And, as in the case of other things that which comes into being is not the same, except in kind, as that which has perished, so too (they say) is it with the universes.' Now if the atoms remain the same, being immune from alteration, clearly these thinkers also must be ascribing to the worlds change of quality and not destruction, as Empedocles and Heraclitus seem to do. A few words quoted from Aristotle *On Democritus* will reveal the line of thought of the Atomists:

'Democritus thinks the nature of the eternal entities consists of small substances infinite in number; as a place for them he supposes something else infinite in size, and to this he applies the names "void", "nothing", and "the infinite", while to each of the substances he applies the names "thing", "solid",[1] and "real". He thinks the substances are so small as to escape our senses, but have all sorts of shapes and figures, and differences of size. From these substances, as from elements, are generated and compounded visible and sensible masses. The substances are at variance and move in the void because of their dissimilarity and the other aforesaid differences, and as they move they impinge on each other and are so completely interlocked that they touch one another or get near one another; but a single substance is never in reality produced from them by this interlocking; for it would be very naïf to suppose that two or more things

[1] Reading in R. 166. 5 τῷ δὲν καὶ τῷ ναστῷ, with Heiberg.

could ever become one. The fact that substances stay with one another for some time the Atomists ascribe to the bodies fitting into one another and catching hold of one another; for some of them are scalene, others hook-shaped, others concave, others convex, and others have numberless other differences. He thinks they cling to one another and remain together until some stronger force arriving from the environment shakes them asunder and separates them.'

He ascribes the genesis and the separation opposed to it not only to animals but also to plants and to worlds, and comprehensively to all sensible bodies. If, then, genesis is combination of atoms, and destruction separation of them, then even according to Democritus 'genesis' must be change of quality. Indeed, Empedocles, too, says that that which comes into being is not the same, except in kind, with that which has perished, and yet Alexander says that Empedocles assumes the existence of change of quality, not of coming into being.

AUTHORS QUOTED

(*a*) = not in Rose. (*b*) = not in Walzer.
(*c*) = fuller quotation than Rose gives.

Ael. *V.H.* 2. 26 134
4. 17 . . . . 135. 139
al-Dailami, cod. Tüb. Weisweiler 81 (*a*) . . 26
Alex. Aph.
in Metaph. 38. 8–41. 15 (*c*) 141
55. 20–57. 28 (*c*) . . 117
59. 28–60. 2 . . . 122
75. 15–17 . . . 141
79. 3–83. 30 (*c*) . . 125
83. 34–89. 7 (*c*) . . 129
85. 16–18 . . . 119
97. 27–98. 24 . . 132
117. 23–118. 1 (*a*, *b*) . 83
250. 17–20 . . . 122
250. 17–19 (*a*) . . 109
262. 18–26 . . . 122
in Top. 5. 17–19 . . 103
27. 11–18 . . . 103
62. 30–63. 19 . . 104
149. 9–17 . . . 27
242. 1–9 . . . 105
apud Eliam *in Cat.* 115. 3–5 5
apud Simp. *in Phys.* 454. 19–455. 11 (*a*) . . 119
al-Kindī,
cod. Aya Sofia 4832, fol. 34b (*a*, *b*) 23
cod. Taimuriyye Falsafa 55 (*a*, *b*) 23
Amm. *in Cat.* 6. 25–7. 4 (*c*) . 5
13. 20–25 . . . 107
Apollon. *Mirab.* 6 . . 134
25 11
Apul. *De Deo Soc.* 20. 166–7 . 137
Arist.
De An. $404^{b}16$–24 (*a*, *b*) . 83
$404^{b}16$–21 (*a*) . . 116
$404^{b}18$–21 (*a*) . . 1
Metaph. $1003^{b}33$–$1004^{a}2$ (*a*) 109
$1054^{a}29$–32 (*a*) . . 109
Ph. $194^{a}27$–36 (*a*) . . 99
$194^{a}35$–36 (*a*) . . 1
$209^{b}11$–16 (*a*) . . 115
Poet. $1454^{b}15$–18 (*a*) . . 1, 72
Aristox. Harm. 2. 30. 16–31. 3 (*a*) 115
Asc. *in Metaph.* 77. 2–4 (*a*) . 116
79. 7–10 (*a*) . . . 123
112. 16–19 (*a*, *b*) . . 78
237. 11–14 (*a*) . . 122
237. 11–13 (*a*) . . 109
247. 17–19 (*a*) . . 122
Ath. 6 d. 63
34 b 13
40 c–d 9
44 d 11
178 e–f. 8
335 f 52
354 c 64
429 c–d 13
429 f 13
447 a–b 12
464 c–d 14
496 f 14
505 b–c 73
555 d–556 a 61
564 b 25
641 b 12
641 d–e 12
674 e–675 a 9
August.
C. Jul. Pel. 4. 14. 72 (*a*) . 101
4. 15. 78 . . . 41
Trin. 14. 9. 12 . . . 46
14. 19. 26 . . . 42
Basil, Ep. 135 5
Boeth.
Consol. 3. 8 . . . 40
in Cat. 1. 161 d–162 a . 108
Censor. c. 18. 11 . . . 55
Chalc. *in Tim.* 208–9 (*b*, *c*) . 53
Cic.
Acad. 1. 7. 26 (*a*) . . 98
Att. 4. 16. 2 . . . 3
12. 40. 2 . . . 65
13. 19. 3–4 . . . 3
13. 28. 2 . . . 65
Brut. 31. 120–1 (*a*) . . 2

Cic. (*cont.*)
De Or. 1. 11. 49 (*a*) . . 1
3. 21. 80 (*a*) . . . 1
Div. ad Brut. 1. 25. 53 . 16
1. 30. 63 (*a*) . . . 84
Fam. 1. 9. 23 (*a*) . . 3
Fin. 2. 13. 39–40 . . 42
2. 32. 106 . . . 53
5. 4. 11 . . . 68
5. 5. 12–14 (*a*) . . 54
5. 5. 12 . . . 2
Hortensius, fr. 35 . . 55
fr. 81 (*a*) . . . 101
Inv. 2. 6 (*a*) . . . 1
Lucullus 38. 119 (*a*) . . 92
N.D. 1. 13. 33 . . . 97
1. 38. 107 . . . 80
2. 15. 42 . . . 93
2. 16. 44 . . . 93
2. 20. 51–2 . . . 55
2. 37. 95–6 . . . 85
Off. 2. 16. 56–7 . . . 57
Q. Fr. 3. 5. 1 . . . 3, 68
Rep. 3. 8. 12 . . . 100
Top. 1. 3 (*a*) . . . 2
Tusc. 1. 10. 22 (*a*) . . 98
1. 17. 41 (*a, b*) . . 98
1. 26. 65–27. 66 (*a*) . 98
1. 39. 94 (*a, b*) . . 40
3. 28. 69 . . . 37
4. 19. 43–20. 46 . . 69
5. 5. 12–14 (*a*) . . 54
5. 10. 30 (*a*) . . . 54
5. 13. 39 (*a*) . . . 54
5. 30. 85–31. 87 (*a*) . 54
5. 35. 101 . . . 53
Clem. Al.
Protr. 1. 7. 4 (*a*) . . 42
Strom. 1. 14. 60. 3 . . 79
1. 14. 61. 1 . . . 79
6. 6. 53. 2–3 . . . 137
6. 18. 162. 5 (*a, b*) . 29
Clem. Rom. *Recogn.* 8. 15 (*a, b*) 99
Cod. Marc. 257, f. 250 . . 105
Damasc. *Pr.* 2. 172. 16–22 . 147
David, *Proll.* 9. 2–12 . . 28
Demetr. *Eloc.* 28 . . . 100
Dexippus *in Cat.* 33. 8–13 . 106
Dio Chr. *Or.* 53. 1 . . . 3, 72
Diog. Laert. 1 Prooem. 8 (6) . 79
2. 5. 23 (7) . . . 78
2. 5. 26 (10) . . . 60
Diog. Laert. (*cont.*)
2. 5. 46 75
2. 6. 55 7
3. 37 (25) 74
3. 48 (32) 73
3. 80 (45) 105
8. 1. 11 (9) 135
8. 1. 19 (18) 138
8. 1. 33–36 (19) . . . 138
8. 2. 51–52 (1) . . . 72
8. 2. 57–58 (3) . . . 72
8. 2. 57 (3) 15
8. 2. 63 (9) 15
8. 2. 74 (11) 73
9. 5. 25 (4) 15
9. 8. 53 (4) 64
9. 8. 54 (5) 15
9. 11. 81 11
Diog. *Oen.* fr. 4 col. 1.7—col.
2.8 4
Dox. Gr. 432. 4–8 (*a*) . . 94
Elias
in Cat. 114. 15–115. 5 (*c*) . 5
114. 25–115. 12 . . 17
124. 3–6 (*a*) . . . 6
133. 9–17 . . . 103
133. 9–17 (*a*) . . . 107
in Porph. 3. 17–23 . . 28
Etymol. Magn. 722. 16–17 . 79
Eus. *P.E.* 14. 6. 9–10 (*a*) . 4
Gell. 3. 11. 7 77
4. 11. 11–13 . . . 137
Greg. Cor. *Ad Hermog.* c. 19 . 100
Hist. Aug. 2. 97. 20–22. . 27
Hom. *Opera*, vol. 5. 244 . 77
247 77
251–2 77
Iambl.
Comm. Math. 26. 79. 1–81.7 . 30
26. 83. 6–22 . . . 37
Myst. 1. 11 74
3. 9 75
Protr. 6. 37. 3–22 (*a*) . 29
6. 37. 26–41. 5 . . 31
7. 41. 15–43. 25 (*a*) . 34
7. 43. 25–45. 3 (*a*) . . 36
8. 45. 4–47. 4 . . . 38
8. 47. 5–21 . . . 39
8. 47. 21–48. 9 . . . 41
8. 48. 9–21 . . . 42
9. 49. 3–52. 16 (*a*) . . 43
9. 52. 16–54. 5 . . . 46

Iambl.—*Protr.* (*cont.*)
10. 54. 10–56. 12 (*a*) . 47
11. 56. 13–59. 18 (*a*) . 49
12. 59. 19–60. 15 (*a*) . 52
V.P. 6. 30–31 136
28. 140–3 135
Jerome, *Adv. Libros Rufini* 3. 39 140
Lact.
Epit. 55 101
Inst. 2. 10. 24 (*a, b*) . . 93
3. 16 29
5. 15 101
Macr. 5. 18. 16–19 . . 75
7. 3. 23 . . . 8
Mart. Cap. 5. 44 (*b*) . . 27
7. 131 . . . 140
Michael Psellus, *Schol. ad Joh. Climacum* 6. 171 (*a*) . 87
Nemes. *De Nat. Hom.* ch. 34 (*a, b*) 94
Nonius 394. 26–28 . . 27
Olymp.
in Alc. p. 144 . . . 28
in Phd. 26. 22–27. 4 . . 94
173. 20–30 . . . 21
180. 22–23 (*a, b*) . . 94
200. 3–6 . . . 94
239. 19–21 . . . 94
Pap. Herc. 1020 (*a*) . . 71
Pap. Oxyrrh. 666 . . 29
Philo,
Aet. Mundi 3. 10–11 . 88
5. 20–24 . . . 89
6. 28–27. 34 . . . 90
8. 39–43 . . . 91
Leg. Alleg. 3. 32. 97–99 . 86
De Plant. 34. 141–40. 166 . 9
De Praem. et Poen. 7. 40–46 87
De Spec. Leg. 1. 35. 185–36. 194 87
Philod.
De Ira, p. 65. 31–66. 2 . 70
Pap. Herc. 3, p. 41, col. 211 (*a*) 57
Piet. 7b4–8 (*a, b*) . . 78
Voll. Rhet. 2. 175 fr. 15. 1–6 (*a*) 71
Philop.
in De An. 75. 34–76. 1 (*a, b*) 84
75. 34–76. 1 . . 116
Philop.—*in De An.* (*cont.*)
141. 22–147. 10 . . 19
186. 14–16 . . . 80
in Nicom. Isagogen, 1. 1 (*a, b*) . . . 80
in Ph. 515. 29–32 (*a*) . 116
in Ph. 521. 9–15 (*a*) . . 115
Pliny, *N.H.* 30. 3 (*a*) . . 79
Plu.
Aristid. 27. 2 60
Dion 22. 3 16
Mor. 115 b–e 18
329 b 67
370 c (*a*) 80
382 d–e (*a, b*) . . . 22
447 f–448 a (*a*) . . . 4
477 c–f (*a*) 87
503 e–504 b 11
527 a 57
612 d–e 8
650 a 13
651 f–652 a (*a*) . . . 14
733 c (*b*) 22
734 d 64
760 e–761 b 25
761 d–e 25
908 f (*a, b*) 94
1040 e 101
1115 b–c (*a*) 82
1115 b–c 4
1118 c 78
1138 c–1140 b . . . 95
Pel. 3. 1 57
18. 4 25
Porph.
apud Stob. 3. 21. 26 . . 78
in De Int. apud Boeth. *in De Int.* 1. 1. p. 27 . 101
V.P. 23–28 136
41 139
42 139
45 137
Prisc. Lydus. 41. 16–42. 3 . 78
Procl.
apud Philop. *De Aet. Mundi*, 31. 17–32. 8 . 82
in Eucl., 28. 13–22 . . 34
90. 14–18 . . . 145
in Remp. 1. 42. 2–50. 26 . 74
2. 349. 13–26 . . 17
in Tim. 61 c . . . 145
338 c–d . . . 17

Ps.-Alex. *in Metaph.* 615. 14–17 (*a*) . . . 122
642. 38–643. 3 (*a*) . . 122
695. 23–6 (*a*). . . 122
777. 16–21 (*a*, *b*) . . 84
836. 34–837. 3 . . 124
Ps.–Amm. *in Cat.* 5 *b* . . 65
9 *b* . . . 65, 67
13 *a* (*a*) . . . 107
17 *a* 108
Ps.-Galen. *Phil. Hist.* c. 35 (*a*, *b*) 94
Ps.-Jul. *Ep.* 391 b–c . . 12
Ps. Plu. *Vit. Hom.* 3–4 . 76
Quint. *Inst.* 2. 17. 1–14 . 7
3. 1. 13 . . . 7
10. 1. 83 (*a*) . . . 3
Schol.
in Aristoph. *Pacem.* 1. 772 12
in *An. Pr.*, cod. Paris. 2064, fol. 263 *a* . . . 28
in *Cat.* 33b25–33 . 108
in Dion. Thrac. 116. 13–16 124
in *Proverb. Sal.* cod. Paris. 174, fol. 46 *a* . . 88
in Theocr. 3. 21 . . 9
Sen.
Brev. Vit. 1. 2. (*a*, *b*) . 41
De Ira 1. 3. 3 . . . 68
1. 7. 1 69
1. 9. 2 68
1. 17. 1 . . . 69
3. 3. 1 69
Q.N. 7. 30 . . . 87
Serv. in *Aen.* 6. 448 (*a*, *b*) . 23
Sext. Emp. *Dogm.* 1. 6–7 . 15
Geom. 57 121
Phys. 1. 20–23 . . . 84
1. 26–27 . . . 85
1. 412 121
2. 45–46 (*a*) . . . 82
Pyrr. 1. 84 . . . 11
Simp.
in Cat. 4. 14–22 (*a*) . . 5
18. 16–21 . . . 107
64. 18–65. 10 . . 106
65. 4–8 (*a*) . . . 105
382. 7–10 (*a*) . . 109
387. 17–388. 14 . . 110
388. 21–389. 10 . . 111
389. 25–390. 7 . . 111
390. 19–25 . . . 112
402. 26–403. 24 . . 112
Simp.—*in Cat.* (*cont.*)
407. 15–20 . . . 109
409. 15–410. 30 . . 113
in De An. 28. 7–9 (*a*) . 83
28. 7–9 116
53. 1–4 21
221. 20–33 . . . 22
in De Caelo
288. 31–289. 2 (*a*, *b*) . 5, 78
289. 1–15 . . . 87
294. 23–295. 26 . . 148
296. 16–18 . . . 147
386. 9–23 . . . 141
392. 16–32 . . . 145
485. 19–22 . . . 58
511. 25–512. 14 . . 145
in Ph. 151. 6–19 (*c*) . . 119
453. 25–454. 19 . . 120
454. 19–455. 11 (*a*) . 119
503. 10–15 (*a*) . . 116
542. 9–12 (*a*) . . 116
545. 23–25 (*a*) . . 116
1355. 8–9 (*a*) . . 145
Sophon. *in De An.* 25. 4–8 (*a*) . 22
Stob. 1. 18. 1c . . . 141
1. 26. 3 146
1. 43 (*a*) . . . 94
3. 3. 25 29
4. 29 A 24 . . . 59
4. 29 A 25 . . . 59
4. 29 C 52 . . . 61
4. 32. 21 . . . 27
Strabo 1. 4. 9, p. C 66 . . 67
14. 5. 9, p. C 672 (*a*) . 53
Suet. *De Blasph.* p. 416 . 100
Suidas, s.v. *Εὐρύβατος* . . 100
Synes.
Calvit. Enc. 22. 85 c . . 80
Dio. 10. 48 a . . . 87
Syr. *in Metaph.* 61. 12–17 (*a*) 109
120. 33–121. 4 . . 124
159. 33–160. 5 . . 82
168. 33–35 . . . 68
195. 10–15 . . . 124
Tac. *Dial.* 16. 7 (*a*) . . 55
Tert. *De An.* 46 (*a*, *b*) . . 55
Them.
in De An. 24. 13–25. 25 . 21
106. 29–107. 5 . . 16
in De Caelo 96. 17–22 . 146
in Ph. 106. 21–23 (*a*) . 115

Them. (*cont.*)
Or. 26 d–27 b . . 101
107 c–d . . . 66
295 c–d . . . 24
319 c 5
Theo. Sm. 21. 20–22. 9 . 140
Theon, *Prog.* 2. 165 . . 103
Vit. Arist. Marc. 427. 3–7 . 72
430. 15–431. 2 . . 65
433. 10–15 . . 116
vulgo 72
Vitae Homeri in *Homeri Opera*, ed. Allen, 5. 244. 247. 251–2 . . . 77

ROSE'S NUMBERING OF FRAGMENTS

R^3	R^2	*Trans., p.*	R^3	R^2	*Trans., p.*	R^3	R^2	*Trans., p.*
1	4	78	54	..	53	104	100	12
2	3	78	55	..	38	105	218	12
3	5	78	56	86	57	106	101	12
4	6	79	57	89	29	107	102	13
5	7	79	58	..	46	108	103	13
6	8, 29	79	59	49	39	109	104	13
7	9	80	60	36	41	110–11	105–6	14
8	10	82	61	48	42	112	109	104
9	11	82	62	51	64	113	110	105
10	12	84	63	52	64	114	111	105
11	13	85	64	53	24	115	112	105
12	14	85	65	54	15	116	113	106
13	2	80	66	55	15	117	114	107
14	44	87	67	56	15	118	115	110
15	45	87	68	57	7	119	116	111
16	15	87	69	58	7	120	117	111
17	16	88	70	59	72	121	118	112
18	17	88	71	60	72	122–3	119–20	112
19	..	89	72	61	73	124	121	113
20	..	90	73	62	74	139	133	7
21	..	91	74	64	75	185	180	124
22	18	92	75	65	75	186	181	124
23–24	19–20	93	76	66	76	187	182	125
25	..	55	78	70	68	188	183	129
26	21	97	79	..	68	189	184	132
27	22	116	80	94–95	68	191	186	134
28	23	117	81	63	74	192	187	136
29	24	121	82	71	100	193	188	137
30	25	122	83	72	63	194	189	137
31	26	122	84	73	100	195	190	138
37	32	16	85	74	101	196	191	139
38	33	16	86	75	101	197	192	139
39	33	17	87	76	101	198	193	140
40	34	17	88	..	101	199	194	140
41	35	17	89	87	57	200	195	141
42	37	94	90	77	52	201	196	141
43	38	22	91	82	59	202	197	141
44	40	18	92	83	59	203	198	141
45	41	19	93	84	60	204	199	145
46	42	22	94	85	61	205	200	145
47	43	95	96	91	25	206	..	147
48	39	94	97	92	25	207	201	147
49	46	58	98	93	25	208	202	148
50	47	27	100	175	8	646	78	65
51	50	27	101	108	9	647	79	66
52	..	30	102	98	9	648	80	67
53	1	37	103	99	11	658	81	67

BIBLIOGRAPHY

ROSE, V., *Aristoteles Pseudepigraphus*, 1863.

——, *Aristotelis qui ferebantur Librorum Fragmenta* [1870].

——, *Aristotelis qui ferebantur Librorum Fragmenta*, 1886.

HEITZ, E., *Aristotelis Fragmenta*, 1872.

WALZER, R., *Aristotelis Dialogorum Fragmenta*, 1934.

ALBEGGIANI, F., Aristotele e Epicuro, in *Logos*, 1937, 422–4.

BERNAYS, J., Aus dem aristotelischen Dialog Eudemos, in *Rhein. Mus.*, 1861, 236–46.

——, *Die Dialoge des Aristoteles*, 1863.

BIDEZ, J., A propos d'un Fragment retrouvé de l'Aristote perdu, in *Bull. de la Cl. des Lettres de l'Acad. Roy. de Belgique*, 1942, 201–30.

——, Hermias d'Atarnée, ibid., 1943, 133–46.

——, *Un Singulier Naufrage littéraire dans l'antiquité*, 1943.

BIGNONE, E. Nuove ricerche e testimonianze sulla prima dottrina e sulle opere perdute di Aristotele attraverso gli scritti degli Epicurei, in *Rivista di Filologia*, 1933, 16–43, 155–76.

——, Nuove ricerche sulla formazione filosofica di Epicuro, in *Atene e Roma*, 1933, 13–62, and *Annali della R. Scuola Normale Superiore di Pisa*, 1933, 273–300, 333–58, and 1934, 289–330.

——, Alla riconquista dell' Aristotele perduto, in *Giornale critico della Filosofia italiana*, 1934, 13–58.

——, La polemica di Epicuro in difesa dell' edonismo, contro le opere perdute di Aristotele e della scuola platonico-peripatetica, in *Atene e Roma*, 1934, 3–62, 129–61.

——, La formazione dell' etica Epicurea attraverso la polemica con il primo Aristotele e la scuola Platonico-Aristotelica, ibid., 1934, 217–311, and 1935, 3–52.

——, Una nuova meta nella riconquista dell' Aristotele perduto, in *Civiltà Moderna*, 1935, 117 ff.

——, Il *Simposio* di Aristotele e quello di Epicuro, in *Atti del IV° Congresso intern. di Papirologia*, 1936, 123–58.

——, *L'Aristotele perduto e la Formazione filosofica di Epicuro*, 2 vols. [1936].

——, Nuove testimonianze e frammenti del *Protrettico* di Aristotele, in *Riv. di Fil. Class.*, 1936, 225–37.

——, Chiarimenti e aggiunte all' *Aristotele perduto*, in *Atene e Roma*, 1937, 119–29.

——, Conferme ed aggiunte all' *Aristotele perduto*, in *Ann. de l'Inst. de Phil.*, 1937, 87–116.

——, Importanti conferme all' *Aristotele perduto*, in *Atene e Roma*, 1937, 217–34.

BIGNONE, E., Aristotele e Diogene di Enoanda, ibid., 1938, 214–32.

——, Postilla aristotelica sulla dottrina dell' endelecheia, ibid., 1940, 61–64.

——, Seneca, Marco Aurelio e il *Protrettico* di Aristotele, in *Ann. d. Sc. Norm. Sup. di Pisa*, 1940, 241–9.

BOURNOT, W. *Platonica Aristotelis Opuscula*, Putbus, 1853.

BYWATER, I., On a lost dialogue of Aristotle [the Protrepticus], in *Journal of Philol.*, 1869, 55–69.

——, Aristotle's dialogue *On Philosophy*, ibid., 1877, 64–87.

CAPONE-BRAGA, G., Aristotele, Epicuro e Diogene di Enoanda, in *Atene e Roma*, 1940, 35–47.

CATAUDELLA, Q., Nuove ricerche sull' Anonimo di Giamblico e sulla composizione del *Protrettico*, in *R. Accad. d. Linzei, Rendici cl. sc. mor.*, 1937–8, 182–210.

COURCELLE, P., *Les Lettres grecques en Occident, de Macrobe à Cassiodore*, 1943.

DIELS, H., Über die exoterischen Reden des Aristoteles, *Ber. Berl. Akad.*, 1883, 477–94.

——, Zu Aristoteles' *Protreptikos* u. Cicero's *Hortensius*, in *Archiv f. Gesch. d. Philos.*, 1888, 477–97.

DYROFF, A., Über Arist. Entwicklung, in *Festgabe für Georg v. Hertling*, 1913.

EINARSON, B., On a supposed pseudo-Aristotelian treatise on the soul, in *Class. Philol.*, 1933, 129–30.

——, Aristotle's *Protrepticus* and the structure of the *Epinomis*, in *Trans. of the Amer. Philos. Association*, 1936, 261–85.

FESTUGIÈRE, A. J., *L'Idéal religieux des Grecs et l'Évangile*, 1932, 222–63.

——, *La Révélation d'Hermès Trismégiste*, 1949, ii. 219–59, 587–91 (on the *De Philosophia*).

GADAMER, H. Der aristotelische *Protreptikos* u. d. entwicklungsgeschichtliche Betrachtung d. Arist. Ethik, in *Hermes*, 1928, 138–64.

GARIN, E., *'Ενδελεχεία* e *'Εντελεχεία* nelle discussioni umanistiche, in *Atene e Roma*, 1937, 177–87.

GUTHRIE, W. K. C., The Development of Aristotle's Theology, in *Cl. Qu.*, 1933, 161–71.

HARDER, R., *Ocellus Lucanus*, 1926, pp. 22, 122–5.

HARTLICH, De exhortationibus a Graecis Romanisque scriptis historia, in *Leipz. Stud. z. klass. Philol.*, 1889, 236–72.

HEITZ, E., *Die verlorenen Schriften des Aristoteles*, 1865.

HIRZEL, R., Über den *Protreptikos* des Arist., in *Hermes*, 1876, 61–100.

——, Ueber Entelechie u. Endelechie, in *Rhein. Mus.*, 1884, 169–208.

JAEGER, W., *Aristoteles: Grundlegung einer Geschichte seiner Entwicklung*, 1923.

—— ——, trans. by R. Robinson, 1934, 1948.

JAEGER, W., Ἀπαρχαί, in *Hermes*, 1929, 22–23.

KAIL, A., De Aristotelis dialogis, qui inscribuntur *De Philosophia* et *Eudemus*, in *Dissert. Philol. Vindob.*, 1913, 67–99.

KARPP, H., Die Schrift des Aristoteles *Περὶ Ἰδεῶν*, in *Hermes*, 1933, 384–91.

LAZZATI, G., L'Aristotele perduto e gli scrittori cristiani, in *Pubbl. d. Univ. Catt.*, 1938.

MANSION, S., Deux écrits de jeunesse d'Aristote sur la doctrine des Idées, in *Rev. Philos. de Louvain*, 1950, 398–416.

MARIOTTI, S., Un passo di Servio e l'*Eudemo* di Aristotele, in *Studi ital. di Filol. Cl.*, 1938, 83–85.

——, Cicerone e una fonte stoica dipendente da Aristotele, in *Stud. ital. di Filol. Cl.*, 1940, 73–76.

——, Nuove testimonianze ed echi dell' Aristotele giovanile, in *Atene e Roma*, 1940, 48–60.

——, La 'quinta essentia' nell' Aristotele perd. e nell. Accademia, in *Riv. di Filol.*, 1940, 179–89.

MUGNIER, H., *La Théorie du premier Moteur et l'Évolution de la Pensée aristotélicienne*, 1930.

NEEDLER, M. C., The Aristotelian *Protrepticus* and the developmental treatment of the Aristotelian ethics, in *Class. Phil.*, 1928, 280–4.

NORSA, M., Un frammento di fisica aristotelica in uno papiro fiorentino, in *Annali della R. Scuola Normale Superiore di Pisa*, 1938, 1–12.

OELLACHER, H., Griechische literarische papyri aus der Papyrussammlung Erzherzog Rainer in Wien, in *Études de Papyrologie*, 1937, 135–96.

ORTH, E., Ein neues aristotel. fragment, in *Philol. Wochenschr.*, 1934, 589–90.

PHILIPPSON, R., Il *Περὶ Ἰδεῶν* di Aristotele, in *Riv. di Filol.*, 1936, 13–25.

——, Diogene di Enoanda e Aristotele, ibid., 1938, 235–52.

POHLENZ, M., Review of Walzer's *Aristotelis Dialogorum Fragmenta*, in *Gött. Gelehrte Anzeiger*, 1936, 514–31.

ROSTAGNI, A., Il dialogo *Περὶ Ποιητῶν*, in *Riv. di Fil.*, 1926, 433–70, and 1927, 145–73.

——, Qualche osservazioni supra un papiro estetico-letterario attribuito ad Aristotele, ibid., 1938, 295–7.

SHOREY, P., Les Idées de Platon et l'évolution d'Aristote, in *Mélanges Paul Thomas*, 1930, 133–49.

VON ARNIM, H., *Quellenstudien zu Philo von Alexandria*, 1888, pp. 5–8.

VON DER MÜHLL, P., Isokrates u. d. *Protreptikos* des Aristoteles, in *Philol.*, 1941, 259–65.

WALZER, R., Un frammento nuovo di Aristotele, in *Studi ital. di Filol. Class.*, 1937, 125–37.

WALZER, R., Fragmenta graeca in litteris arabicis, in *Journal of the Royal Asiatic Society*, 1939, 407–22.

WASZINK, J. H., Traces of Aristotle's lost dialogues in Tertullian, in *Vigiliae Christianae*, 1947.

——, art. Aristoteles, in *Reallexikon f. Antike u. Christentum*, i. 657–64.

WILPERT, P., Reste verlorener aristotelischer aristotelesschriften bei Alexander von Aphrodisias, in *Hermes*, 1940, 369–96.

——, P., Neue Fragmente aus *Περὶ Τἀγαθοῦ*, in *Hermes*, 1941, 225–50.

——, *Zwei aristotelische Frühschriften über die Ideenlehre*, 1949.

ZÜRCHER, J., *Aristoteles' Werk u. Geist*, 1952, pp. 21–31.

INDEX

Academy, x.
Alexamenos, 73–74.
Alexander the Great, ix, xi, 65, 67.
Alexander, viii, ix, x, xi, 67.
Anger, 68–71.
Antisthenes, xi.
Archytas, 109–10, 147.
Archytas, On the Philosophy of, 147.
Aristotle's style, 1, 2, 3, 5, 6, 92–93; open-mindedness, 4; attitude to Plato, 4.
Art and nature, 43–46.

Bignone, E., xii.

Categories, 107–8.
Cicero, viii, x, xii.
Colonists, On, viii, ix.
Contraries, On, 109–14.
Corinthian dialogue, viii, 24.

Delphi, 78–79.
Democritus, On, 148–9.
Deucalion, 81.
Dialogues, Aristotle's, vii–xii, 1–6.
Diogenes Laertius, vii, viii, xi.
Dissertations, 106.
Divisions, 105.
Dreams, 55–56.
Drinking and Drunkenness, 8–14.
Drunkenness, On, vii, n. 7.

Education, On, viii, ix, 64.
Einarson, B., x.
Empedocles, 15, 72–73.
Eroticus, vii, ix, 25–26.
Eudemus, 16.
Eudemus, vii, n. 8, viii, ix, xi, xii, 16–23.
Eudoxus, 132.
Euripides, 75.
Euthydemus, x, n. 1.
Exoteric works, 5, 6.

Fifth element (ἀκατονόμαστον), 98–99.
Forms, Platonic, 22.

Good, On the, viii, xi, 115–23.
Good Birth, On, vii, viii, ix, 59–62.

Gorgias, x.
Great year, 55.
Gryllus, vii, 7.
Gryllus, vii, ix, 7.

Happiness, 54–55.
Hermippus, vii.
Hesychius, vii, viii, xi.
Homer, 8–9, 72, 76–77, 84–85.
Hortensius, viii, 27.
Howald, E., vii.

Ideal numbers, xi.
Ideas, Platonic, xi, xii, 117, 124–33.
Ideas, On, xi, xii, 124–33.
Immortality, 16–18.
Indefinite dyad, 117–21, 123.
Isocrates, x.

Jaeger, W., ix, xi, xii.
Justice, On, vii, ix, 100–2.

Kingship, On, viii, ix, x, xi, 65–66.

Love, 25–26.

Magi, 79–80.
Magicus, xi.
Mathematics, 30–31, 34.
Melissus, 82.
Menexenus, vii, ix.
Metaphysics, xii.
Music, 95–97.
Mysteries, the, 87.

Nerinthus, vii, viii, ix, 24.
Numbers, 117–19.

One and indefinite dyad, 117–21, 123; One and Plurality, 122.

Parmenides, 82.
Parts of speech, 106.
Phaedo, x, n. 1.
Philosophy, 27–30, 33–34, 37, 52.
Philosophy, On, vii, viii, ix, x, xi, xii, 78–99.
Plato, ix, x, xi, 74, 82–84, 88, 115–33.

Pleasure, On, viii, ix, 63.
Poets, On, vii, viii, ix, 72–77.
Politicus, vii, viii, ix, x, 68–71.
Prayer, On, vii, ix, 58.
Privation, 112–13.
Problems, On, 104.
Protrepticus, vii, viii, ix, x, n. 1, xii, 27–56.
Pseudo-Ammonius, xi.
Pythagoras, 134–9.
Pythagoreans and numbers, 117, 140–5; and cosmology, 145–6.
Pythagoreans, On the, xii, 134–46.

Religion, origin of, 84–87.
Rhetoric, 1.
Rhetoric, On, vii, 7.
Rose, V., xi, xii.

Sardanapallus, 52–53.
Sophistes, vii, ix, 15.
Soul and body, 17–22, 32, 34.
Soul, On, vii, viii, 16–23.
Stage-effect, 1.
Strabo, xi.
Suidas, xi.
Symposium, vii, ix, 8–14.

Themison, 27.
'Third man', 129.

Von der Mühll, P., x.

Walzer, R., xii.
Wealth, On, vii, ix, 57.
Wilpert, P., xi, xii.
World, ungenerated and imperishable, 88–93.

Zoroaster, 79–80.